RULES OF PRINTED ENGLISH

HERBERT REES

Rules of Printed English

LONDON
DARTON, LONGMAN & TODD

First published in 1970 by
Darton, Longman & Todd Ltd
64 Chiswick High Road, London W.4

SBN 232 51038 5

Printed in Great Britain by
Alden & Mowbray Ltd
at the Alden Press, Oxford

CONTENTS

PREFACE

Rules of printed English? What impertinence!—until you reflect that rules are not dogmas, and that every rule is meant to be broken—some time or another.

You will find, for instance, in the following pages that (i) some words are to be ended in –ize: a rule; (ii) others are never on any account to be ended in –ize: a dogma. If you like, you may end them all in –ise; but, whatever you do, you mustn't end them all in –ize.

If you are an author, you are free to choose your own style; you may even have dogmas. One popular writer of eighteenth-century romantic fiction will have *advertize* so spelt to suit the period. Another author will have it that *gray* and *grey* represent two distinct colours. Very well, each must have her way. If you are an editor, you will have to consider your author's dogmas with respect, and occasionally maybe you will wean him from one or two of them—with respect. If you are a printer, you will have to print what you are sent to print, though even then you may gently remind editor or author of what you think one or other of them *may* have overlooked. But all with respect—and no dogmas.

Of course the rules set out here cannot hope to be totally comprehensive. Certain registered trade names with a claim in law to initial capital letters are mentioned (see **193**); but the list is not complete: there are others. Certain foreign words commonly set in roman type are listed (see **241**); again the list is not complete. Spellings may be simply 'preferred' (see **299**), or they may be without alternative (see **300**).

Some of the rules will appear absurdly elementary; others may seem to aim at a somewhat rarefied perfection of style.

All have been shown by experience to be worth formulating. They are not someone else's decisions imposed at will. They seek only to remind the user of this book of the need for decision one way or the other.

HERBERT REES

18 Tory
Bradford-on-Avon

I A SHORT LIST OF USEFUL BOOKS

This list is not a complete bibliography, but consists mainly of small, handy books, especially those available in paperback editions.
References and book lists for further study will be found in many of the works cited here. Short titles are given in brackets for reference elsewhere in the present work.
Divisions are in order of their probable use in the preparation of a manuscript. Within each division, elementary works precede those more advanced.
Asterisks indicate works of especial usefulness or importance.

DICTIONARIES OF ENGLISH 1

* *Chambers's Twentieth Century Dictionary* William Geddie (ed.), rev. edn with Supplement (W. & R. Chambers Ltd, Edinburgh and London 1959) [CHAMBERS]
A full, up-to-date dictionary, with good coverage of American usage and scientific terms. Reliable on alternative spellings, but gives 'ise' endings exclusively.

Concise Oxford Dictionary of Current English, The H. W. and F. G. Fowler (eds), 5th edn, rev. E. McIntosh (Clarendon Press, Oxford 1964)
Based on *The Oxford English Dictionary*. Fewer entries than CHAMBERS; more detailed etymologies.

* ROGET, Peter Mark *Thesaurus of English Words and Phrases* new edn, rev. Robert A. Dutch (Longmans, London 1962); abridged edn (Penguin, Harmondsworth 1953)
The converse of a dictionary: words classified according to *meaning*, 'so as to facilitate the expression of ideas and to assist in literary composition'.

Webster's New World Dictionary of the American Language College edn, illustrated (World Publishing Co., Cleveland and New York 1964)

American College Dictionary, The (Random House, New York 1962)

WEST, Michael *A Dictionary of Spelling, British and American* (Longmans, London 1964)
A handy, up-to-date paperback, making consultation of a big dictionary merely for American spellings unnecessary.

Further dictionaries will, of course, be required for languages other than English, and for specialized subject fields.

2 GENERAL REFERENCE

Whitaker's Almanack (London annually); a shorter paper-bound edition omits details of foreign countries and directory section.

Penguin Encyclopedia, The—paperback, ed. Sir John Summerscale (Penguin, Harmondsworth 1965)
An up-to-the-minute one-volume deskbook, particularly thorough on science and technology.

Oxford Dictionary of Quotations, The 2nd (rev.) edn (Oxford University Press, London 1953)
Reliable texts and references.

Concise Oxford Dictionary of Quotations, The—paperback (Oxford University Press, London 1964)
Competitive with the similar Penguin Dictionary.

* *Who's Who* (A. & C. Black, London annually)

* *Who was Who*: I *1897–1915*; II *1916–1928*; III *1929–1940*; IV *1941–1950*; V *1951–1960* (A. & C. Black, London)
These give final details and date of death.

HYAMSON, Albert A. *A Dictionary of Universal Biography of All Ages and of All Peoples* 2nd (rev.) edn (Routledge & Kegan Paul, London 1951)
A simple name and date list, but useful for checking the identity and period of the most obscure historical persons. References are given to biographies. Not entirely reliable on spelling or dates. Does not include living persons.

* *Webster's Biographical Dictionary* (G. & C. Merriam Co., Springfield, Mass., U.S.A. 1960)

* *Webster's Geographical Dictionary* (G. & C. Merriam Co., Springfield, Mass., U.S.A. 1960)
These two works, up-to-date, encyclopedic, and wholly reliable, are procurable in Britain from G. Bell & Sons Ltd, York House, Portugal Street, London W.C.2. The *Biographical Dictionary* includes living persons, and a useful appendix of successions of historical persons from ancient Egypt to the present day.

* *The Times Index-Gazetteer of the World* (The Times Publishing Co. Ltd, London 1965)

Gazetteer of the British Isles 9th edn (Bartholomew & Son Ltd, Edinburgh 1963)
Gives name of every town, village, hamlet and geographical feature throughout the British Isles, including Eire. Incorporates a summary of the 1961 Census, and provides details of population, situation, postal, railway and other information. Not entirely up-to-date, nor wholly reliable on spelling.

* *Complete Atlas of the British Isles* (The Reader's Digest Association Ltd, London 1965)
Includes a Gazetteer of 32,000 places and features. Reliable on spelling.

The Times Atlas 5 vols (The Times Publishing Co. Ltd, London 1955–9)

3 ENGLISH LANGUAGE AND STYLE

VALLINS, G. H. *Good English: how to write it*—paperback (Pan, London 1951); new, enlarged and revised (hardback) edn (Deutsch, London 1952)
A useful introductory book.

* FOWLER, H. W. *A Dictionary of Modern English Usage* 2nd edn, rev. Sir Ernest Gowers (Oxford University Press, Oxford 1965) [FOWLER]
The classic guide to points of grammar, syntax and style, alphabetically arranged for easy reference. See also NICHOLSON, below.

TREBLE, H. A. and VALLINS, G. H. *An ABC of English Usage* (Oxford University Press, London 1936)
A dictionary of grammar and usage. The English Language Book Society edition (paperback, not available in U.K.) is a cheap alternative to FOWLER for overseas readers. Still useful in spite of its date.

* PARTRIDGE, Eric *Usage and Abusage: a guide to good English* 6th edn (Hamish Hamilton, London 1965); paperback edn (Penguin, Harmondsworth 1963)
Complements FOWLER, but may also be used as an independent alternative.

FOLLETT, Wilson *Modern American Usage* Jacques Barzun (ed.), (Hill & Wang, New York 1966; Longmans, London 1966) [FOLLETT]
Discursive and scholarly.

NICHOLSON, Margaret *A Dictionary of American-English Usage* (Oxford University Press, New York 1957); 'Signet' paperback edn (New American Library, New York 1958) [NICHOLSON]
Based on FOWLER, this adaptation retains much of the original, but condenses, adds new entries, and includes American usage. A very good cheap alternative to FOWLER and FOLLETT combined.

PUNCTUATION 4

CAREY, G. V. *Mind the Stop: a brief guide to punctuation*—paperback, 2nd (rev.) edn (Cambridge University Press, London 1958)
A useful introduction to the subject.

PARTRIDGE, Eric *You have a Point There*—paperback edn (Hamish Hamilton, London 1964)
A comprehensive and reliable guide to punctuation, with a chapter on American practice by John W. Clark, University of Minnesota. Also available in hard covers.

COPY PREPARATION AND PROOF CORRECTION 5

* COLLINS, F. Howard *Authors' and Printers' Dictionary: a guide for authors, editors, printers, correctors of the press, compositors and typists* 10th edn (Oxford University Press, London 1956) [COLLINS]
Pocket size (7″ × 4″). Indispensable as an authority on a wide variety of doubtful points.

* HART, Horace *Rules for Compositors and Readers at the University Press, Oxford* 37th edn (Oxford University Press, London 1967) [HART]
Widely accepted as authoritative. Newly revised throughout and re-set in the same format as COLLINS.

Successive editions of both these works have been modified in accordance with changes in usage, but neither is to be regarded as infallible. In some matters they disagree: e.g. imprimatur (rom., COLLINS); *imprimatur* (ital., HART). In others, again, they are both unduly conservative: e.g. in printing full points after contractions (see **265**).

BRITISH STANDARD 1219 *Recommendations for Proof Correction and Copy Preparation*—pamphlet (British Standards Institution, London 1958)
Refers also to other British Standards of value in copy preparation.

CAREY, G. V. *Making an Index*—pamphlet, 3rd edn, Cambridge Authors' and Printers' Guides (Cambridge University Press, Cambridge 1963)
By a former President of the Society of Indexers. One of a useful series of pamphlets.

6 TYPOGRAPHY

MORISON, Stanley *First Principles of Typography*—pamphlet, Cambridge Authors' and Printers' Guides (Cambridge University Press, Cambridge 1967)
The 1967 reprint of this classic essay contains a hitherto unavailable postscript.

* SIMON, Oliver *Introduction to Typography* David Bland (ed.), (Faber, London 1963)
A valuable guide to book typography, available in both hardback and paperback editions. Helpful book list and glossary.

* BIGGS, John R. *An Approach to Type* 2nd edn (Blandford Press, London 1961)
A useful beginner's book, with many complete sets of type specimens, and an annotated bibliography.

WESTERHAM PRESS *Filmsetting*—pamphlet (Westerham 1963)
'Some suggestions for the use of filmsetting with reflections upon the declining use of hot metal and the opportunity filmsetting offers to the graphic designer.'

Desk books of type specimens from the main typefounders, lists of type held at the printers normally dealt with, and type-specimen tracing sheets for the faces most frequently used are invaluable.

7 BOOK PRODUCTION AND DESIGN

CAMPBELL, G. A. *The Making of a Book* 'Men and Women at Work' series (Oxford University Press, London 1955)

One of an educational paperback series designed to afford practice in English reading, this gives also an illuminating description of book production processes from manuscript to bound copy. Suitable for absolute beginners of all ages.

CLOWES, William *A Guide to Printing: an Introduction for Print Buyers* (Heinemann, London 1963)
A useful handbook for production staff.

* WILLIAMSON, Hugh *Methods of Book Design: the practice of an industrial craft* 2nd (rev.) edn (Oxford University Press, London 1966)
Practises what it preaches: a pleasure to handle. Includes 'some suggestions for authors', useful chapters on text design, and excellent book lists. The glossarial index is a model of its kind.

BIBLIOGRAPHY 8

NATIONAL BOOK LEAGUE *Books about Books*: catalogue of a touring exhibition—pamphlet (National Book League, London 1967)
This catalogue, available on request (price 1*s*.) from 7 Albemarle Street, London W.1, comprises in effect a useful short bibliography of book authorship, design, production, printing, and the book trade. The exhibition is a permanent one, brought up to date annually. It includes only books in print.

COLLISON, Robert L. *Bibliographies, subject and national: a guide to their contents, arrangement and use* 2nd edn (Crosby Lockwood, London 1962)
Besides listing further bibliographies on the book, this is indispensable to the author who wishes to check on work already done in a particular subject field. Usually available in libraries for reference.

2 FULL POINT

9 The full point is mainly used:
(a) to mark the close of a sentence
(b) to end an abbreviation:

Esq. No. i.e. etc. R.A.F.

(c) in decimal coinage:

$14.25

10 The full point should normally be omitted from half-titles, title pages, headlines, running heads, sub-headings, side-headings, and from captions which consist of only a single sentence and in which there is no need to mark off one sentence from another.

(a) The Author in childhood

but: (b) The Author in childhood. His father is seated third from right.

11 A group of three full points separated by en quads (i.e. spaces) indicates an ellipsis (marking the omission of words). This may occur at the beginning, middle, or end of a sentence.

As he passed down the corridor his ears caught the final outburst: ' . . . and if you don't intend to work, get out!'

What I heard between the recurring interruptions of the audience did not tell me what I wanted to know. 'There is one man', the speaker was saying, 'who has defied every attempt to . . . that's all very well,' he shouted angrily, 'you may refuse to listen, but if this damnable scheme has at last been . . . it is owing to the unfailing courage of . . . and to nothing else.' And still I could not hear who it was he was speaking of.

Beside the body lay a scrap of paper with some writing on it: 'This is the only way to . . . '; and he couldn't make out the rest.

12 If the sentence preceding the ellipsis is complete, it will have

its own final full point set close up to the concluding word of the sentence, thus making four consecutive full points in all:

> His thoughts raced on. . . . What on earth was he to do now? If only he had . . . But regrets were useless.

13 The first full point of a 3-point ellipsis should not be set close up to the preceding word; otherwise it will look like the final full point of the preceding sentence. In the above example, both the following would be **wrong**:

(a) His thoughts raced on . . . .
(b) If only he had. . .

14 If a sentence ends with parentheses enclosing a final full point after an abbreviation, it should have its own concluding full point outside the second parenthesis:

> Darius III met his final defeat at the battle of Issus (333 B.C.).

15 Full points are also used, grouped in twos or threes, to lead the eye from one margin of a page or column to the other. These groups are called *leaders*: 2-point groups are to be preferred to 3-point, so as to preserve their distinction from the 3-point ellipsis.

War, Franco-Prussian	242
Water, shortage of	55
Waterloo, numbers engaged at	168

16 Full points are often conventionally printed where, on consideration, they will be seen to be unnecessary. The convention by which a full point would follow the roman numeral after the name of a monarch has now been abandoned. No one would now print **wrongly**:

> Henry VII. was the first of the Tudor line.

But unnecessary full points are still sometimes allowed to spatter a page. Surely *learning their A B C* is preferable to *learning their A.B.C.*

3 COMMA

17 Commas should be used sparingly. If they are too many, they can disfigure the page and obstruct the reader. In the following the comma is superfluous:

Yet, he made no reply. **[wrong]**

Slowly, I came to my senses. **[wrong]**

18 It is sometimes **wrongly** laid down that an inversion of the sentence requires the inserting of a comma, as, for instance:

To all of you, he was very kind. **[wrong]**

The comma here is not only unnecessary; it is obstructive. Contrast the following:

He saw at once that the German and French delegates were present; but the Italian he could not catch sight of.
To the intelligent inquirer he would patiently explain everything.

19 But a comma is often advisable between two proper nouns, where it may ease a momentary confusion in the reader's mind:

On 30 January, Charles was executed.
At Salamis, Xerxes suffered a crushing reverse.

20 In the enumeration of a series, the comma is normally to be omitted before the final *and*, unless it is required to connect two members of the series more closely:

The designs were in red, purple and black.

There were designs in red, purple and black, and green.

She scrubbed every mortal thing she could lay her hands on: the cooker, the sink, the copperware, the pots and pans, and the children's faces into the bargain.

The teaching should be suited to the age, status in the school, and ability of the individual pupil.

Note how the insertion of a comma between two adjectives can effect an important change of meaning: 21

'So they've started a bus service over Harrow Hill, have they? Well, I can recall other, unsuccessful attempts to get that route established.' [The others were unsuccessful; will this be so?]

It would have been premature for the speaker to say:

'Well, I can recall other unsuccessful attempts to . . .',

for the new attempt had not yet proved unsuccessful.

The comma may also be necessary to separate an introductory, or parenthetical, word or phrase from the main sentence and so avoid ambiguity (Imagine the five following sentences without the comma). 22

To start with, the players would be in better form if the tournament could be held later.

He wrote, in all, thirty novels.

Above all, the minor princelings were proving disloyal.

As in a family, no one in the school is given a task beyond his powers.

In all, fifteen ships were acquired.

Contrast: 23

The news gave some hope; still, the outlook remained gloomy.

with:

For all this, there was no real hope; still the outlook remained gloomy.

Contrast:

To begin with, their only means of communication was difficult.

with:

To begin with their only means of communication was difficult.

Further examples of the introductory word or phrase: 24

True, he was over sixty; but he really needn't have retired.

To be sure, the conversation after the ladies had left was deadly boring; however, he consoled himself with the excellent port.

You were brave; what's more, you were a pioneer.

I say, this news is real dynamite!

I tell you, there's trouble ahead of us.

This, however, was certainly not my fault.

However, if you say it was, I shall make no reply.

However you may insist, I shall still say nothing.

25 The comma is frequently used in conversational style to separate two sentences, one of which is dependent on the other:

The fog had grown thicker, he noticed as he set out down the drive.

There was no difference in her tone of voice, of that he was certain.

The memories of that period were more vivid than usual this morning, why he could not tell.

26 It is by no means always correct to precede a relative pronoun or conjunction with a comma. The presence or absence of a comma may subtly affect the meaning.

The epics *Paradise Lost* and *Paradise Regained*, which Milton wrote, are two of the most famous poems in the English language. (*which Milton wrote* here conveys an additional piece of information about the epics which have already been identified by their titles.)

The epics which Milton wrote are named *Paradise Lost* and *Paradise Regained*. (*which Milton wrote* here identifies the epics that are being referred to.)

27 Here is a comma **wrongly** used:

Nearly three centuries had passed since 1666, when the twentieth Lord Suffolk died heroically in 1941.

The comma momentarily misleads the reader into thinking that 1666 was the date when Lord Suffolk died – a false impression which is rectified only when the date of his death appears at the end of the sentence. No such misunderstanding would be created by:

Nearly three centuries had passed since 1666 when the twentieth Lord Suffolk died heroically in 1941.

Two or more adjectives are not to be separated by a comma: 28
(a) if they express between them a single idea:

a good hot dinner (*all the better for being hot*)

a nice sharp walk (*nice because sharp*)

a grand old time

a real old scallywag

a jolly hearty old boy

Contrast:

a mere brief comment (*mere because brief*)

with:

a brief, scathing reply (*the two adjectives express two distinct thoughts: the reply might have been brief but soothing*)

Contrast:

a dear old lady (*her age was what endeared her*)

with:

a lovely, well-dressed woman (*she might have been either; in fact she was both*)

(b) if the last adjective is so closely associated with the noun following it as to form one idea with it: 29

They had some good small talk.

queer, stiff, ugly wax dolls

a modern large-scale organization

a very handsome young man

30 The comma is not always to be placed only in its strictly logical position. A longish or somewhat complicated sentence may include a well-placed comma which is of great assistance to the reader in following the construction:

> But, ever since Ramillies died, every other word that has escaped her, every little offensive trick of mind which she has betrayed and which until now has been muffled by you automatically because her deficiencies were not your affair, has suddenly become italicized.

Note how the comma after *affair* carries the reader's mind at once back to the words early in the sentence – *word, trick* – which are the subjects of the verb *has* which follows the comma.

31 The comma may also be used to link proper names which are associated in some literary, theatrical, or other collaboration:

> the Antony, Octavius, Lepidus scene in Shakespeare's *Julius Caesar*

With a longer series, en rules may be preferable:

> the Sachs–Walther–Eva–David–Magdalene quintet in *Die Meistersinger*

or the solidus may be used, though this is not yet widely accepted:

> the Decca/Solti/Nilsson recording of *Götterdämmerung*

32 A comma may be used to separate reported speech or a question from the main sentence, if the colon would be too formal:

> To the question what was to happen next, the answer seemed to be, Nothing.
>
> The point is, Did you or did you not see the accused that night?
>
> I wondered later, Ought I to have spoken so bluntly?

similarly with a quoted remark:

Over and over again his cry was, 'Excelsior!'

As one Member put it, 'The country is being slowly drained by excessive taxation.'

Note that it is not incorrect in such instances to follow the comma with a capital letter.

The abbreviations, *e.g.*, *i.e.*, *viz.*, should usually be preceded, 33
but not necessarily followed, by a comma:

The syllabus included the masters of English nineteenth-century fiction, e.g. Scott, Dickens, Trollope and others.

the Parish Church of the Commonwealth, i.e. St Paul's Cathedral

He said nothing of the earliest of them all, viz. Chaucer.

A comma should precede *etc.* if more than one item comes 34
before it; *etc.* does not belong to the last member of the series more closely than to any preceding member of it.

Papers etc. were lying about the room.

Papers, pencils, etc. were all over the place.

The comma is required to mark the omission of the verb in 35
the second part of a compound sentence:

To err is human; to forgive, divine.

The comma is also used to mark off a verbal parenthesis, or 36
a word or phrase in apposition:

To be or not to be, that is the question.

His master, El Greco, had influenced him profoundly.

. . . that audacious steel obelisk, the Eiffel Tower

He stopped and, bending down, he gently kissed the child.
(Note that the comma should follow *and*, not precede it.)

You, being a republican, will surely feel the fascination of the trappings of monarchy.

37 The comma, if used with parenthetical phrases such as:

of course after all as it were as a matter of fact say

is required before as well as after them:

He had, of course, heard all about it from me; but you were not, after all, to know that I had had the opportunity of telling him. Well, as a matter of fact, I had made a point of meeting him after church, on Sunday morning. I had, indeed, run him to earth, as it were.

38 But note that the comma is not necessarily used with *of course*:

. . . but of course I know the earth's round.

Who discovered America? Why, Columbus of course.

39 nor necessarily with such parenthetical words as *too*, *indeed*:

This, too, had no influence on government policy.

Then, too, let me add a further point.

but: You can see him; can you see me too?

Funds were desperately low; prices were rising too.

Certain roads should be abandoned too, as not worth their upkeep.

He is not easy to deal with; his attitude is, indeed, entirely negative.

His methods are persuasive; indeed, he makes no explicit demands.

but: He's always indecisive; he has indeed no strong opinions.

40 *Then* has originally a temporal meaning; but when used parenthetically, between commas, it comes to have a purely logical significance.

He had recently resigned from the party. This, then, was his reason for not coming to the meeting.

This then was his reason. Later he would have acted from an entirely different motive.

Finally, it is to be noted that the comma is not used after personal names when they are followed by 'Esq.', 'sen.', 'jun.' or letters of distinction showing degrees, honours, etc. 41

John Smith Esq.

Sir Henry Dale O.M.

Oliver Wendell Holmes jun.

Sir William Temple B[t]

4 COLON

The colon tends to be much neglected: it is either wrongly replaced by the semicolon, which is certainly not its equivalent; or it is simply passed over for a vague and imprecise use of the dash. 42

Use the colon to introduce lists of items: 43

He met everyone there: politicians, churchmen, eminent scientists – in fact, people from all walks of life.

or to introduce sentences enlarging upon an initial comprehensive statement: 44

He had a commanding personality: not only was his presence magnetic, but his voice was so persuasive as to be wellnigh irresistible.

The colon may also be used to introduce further precision in the definition of a topic: 45

Shakespeare's Moral Philosophy: the Problem Plays

World War One: the Somme Offensive

The colon should be used to introduce formal or exact quotation: 46

He ended with the words: 'I have nothing further to say, gentlemen.'

He suddenly shouted: 'Get out of here! Get out, I tell you!'

47 In recording casual conversation, the comma is normally sufficient:

He exclaimed, 'Fancy meeting you!'

but the colon (with no dash following) should be used, if any stop is required, to introduce a quotation beginning on the following line:

and he at once exclaimed, on catching sight of her:
'Fancy meeting you here of all places!'

48 The colon is also used to introduce a formal phrase or question, even if not in quotes:

There is a proverb: Too many cooks spoil the broth.

The password was: Liberty or death.

He put the question straight: Had she seen the thief escaping?

49 But the colon in such instances need not always be followed by a capital letter:

To sum up: you realized you had gone too far.

50 Finally, a well-known use of the colon is to mark a ratio:

2:3 = 4:6   24:36 = 360:540

5 SEMICOLON

51 The semicolon is a middle-weight—half-way between the light-weight comma and the heavy-weight full point. It is used:

(a) to separate two sentences connected in sense but unconnected by a conjunction:

I waited for a reply; he had none to make.

52 (b) to separate consecutive items, numbered or unnumbered, each introduced by a lower-case letter:

There are in the colony three classes of inhabitant: (1) the white people of European descent, whose ancestors of at least three generations have settled and developed the country; (2) the black people, whose ancestors have likewise moved into the country, but from other parts of the African continent; (3) the so-called Coloureds, who are of mixed African and European descent and who stand midway between the two former classes in political representation.

Those who were working for the establishment of a dictatorship could count on the support of the middle classes, who were alarmed at the growing unrest among the unemployed; of the mass of the working class, for whom loyalty to a leader who promised employment was a welcome escape from the grinding frustration of enforced idleness; and of the big business interests, who wished to see discipline imposed on the workers and the return of stable conditions likely to attract foreign investment.

(c) to replace the normal comma where commas are already required in a subordinate position: 53

There were numbers of people, injured and helpless; first-aid men, seeking to alleviate their sufferings; and, in the far distance, ambulance workers with supplies of food and medicine, which they were bringing up with all speed.

6 DASH: EN AND EM RULE

Beware of excessive use of the dash: it is often, like the excessive use of italic, a substitute for clarity of thought. Punctuation, no less than the careful construction of sentences, is an important element of style. 54

When the dash introduces a parenthetical phrase or sentence, it should be provided with its counterpart – a second dash – thus, at the end of the parenthesis. 55

It is undesirable to combine the dash and the colon thus:—. Either the one or the other should be used; not both. 56

The dash should not be preceded or followed by another mark of punctuation. 57

58 The dash may take the form of:

(a) the en rule, of the width of the letter n;*
(b) the em rule, of the width of the letter m;
(c) the 2-em rule, of twice the width of the letter m.

59 (a) The **en rule** should be used to mark off a parenthesis which makes a notable break in the flow of the sentence:

We all – and I really mean all – are on his side.

It may also be used to avoid parentheses within parentheses:

The troops (who were – largely but by no means wholly – drawn from native stock) were loyal to a man.

60 The en rule should be used to join numerals expressing extent of time, distance, age, etc.
Hyphens are *not* to be used for this purpose.

the inter-war years: that is to say, the 1919–39 period	**not:** 1919-39
On that day alone I had walked 12–15 miles.	**not:** 12-15
during the week of 22–27 May	**not:** 22-27
The fullest mental vigour may be found in men of 60–65 years.	**not:** 60-65

61 Note that it is **wrong** to use the en rule in such phrases as *from 12–15 miles*; *from 22–27 May*; *Between 300–1,000 were present.*
The correct form for these phrases is:

from 12 to 15 miles

from 22 to 27 May

Between 300 and 1,000 were present.

62 The use of the hyphen must be clearly distinguished from that of the en rule:

some 11–14-year-old boys

* Note that when the en rule separates, it must be set with a space on either side; when it joins, it must be set without these spaces.

inter-departmental or labour–management relations

The game ended in a 4–1 win for the Rangers. **not:** a 4-1 win

the Jericho–Jerusalem highway

but: the New-Jerusalem Glory

Contrast: the Rome–Berlin Axis

the Franco-German struggle (*one word*)

the Austro-Hungarian Empire (*one word*)

Austria-Hungary (*one political unit*)

Alsace-Lorraine (*one territory*)

Names of joint authors are to be distinguished from hyphenated surnames and should be linked by an en rule: **63**

the Muret–Sanders German dictionary

the Facciolati–Forcellini Latin lexicon

the Toussaint–Langenscheidt method

the Strauss–Hofmannsthal collaboration

the Pauly–Wissowa edition

the R. L. Stevenson–Lloyd Osbourne joint authorship of *The Wrong Box*

The more usual English custom is to use *and* as the link between joint authors' names: **64**

the Liddell and Scott Greek lexicon

the Gilbert and Sullivan operas

the Beaumont and Fletcher plays

The en rule is especially useful to link hyphenated names: **65**

Cahiers de la Compagnie Madeleine Renaud–Jean-Louis Barrault

The en rule is also used to prolong the sound of a word in speech, or to represent a stutter: **66**

'We – ell', he drawled.

'Have you sp – potted my p – pipe anywhere?'

67 (b) The **em rule** is used to mark an interruption or a change of thought:

Why on earth have you — but there! what's the use of arguing?

Vanished! Just as we were about to — Good heavens, there he is again!

68 The em rule is also used for dramatic or rhetorical effect:

Condemned unheard! and they call that — justice.

69 It may also be used before a final phrase or sentence, to sum up previous phrases:

. . . the pursuit of the arts, the rule of law, love of country, reverence for the gods — all this makes up civilization.

70 (c) The **2-em rule** may be used to break off a sentence abruptly and finally:

'Get out, or I'll —— '

'If you only knew —— ', he began. But it was useless to go on.

71 It may also be used to indicate a word or part of a word omitted:

His only reply was a muttered d——.

It was clear that —— had been the victim of blackmail.

And there was Mr A——, as bold as brass, strolling along the esplanade with Mrs B—— on his arm.

'And I don't give a damn for anyone! I'm quite prepared to stand up to His Maj——' He stopped short. The King had entered the room.

7 PARENTHESES

72 Both parentheses and brackets are, of course, found in pairs. Parentheses are rounded; brackets are square-cornered.

73 If the latter of the two parentheses occurs at the end of the sentence, the full point should be outside it:

He remained silent (which I was thankful for).

If the parentheses enclose a complete sentence independent of the preceding sentence, they should enclose the full point also: 74

He cheered up at once. (I was glad to notice it.)

But if the parentheses enclosing a complete sentence are themselves an interjection enclosed in another sentence, they may contain any mark of punctuation proper to their sentence, or none: 75

He cheered up at once (I was glad to notice it) and before long he was singing.

Within a few hours he had completely changed his mind (who would have thought it?) and now wished to withdraw his previous proposal.

A comma or other punctuation mark which would normally follow the word immediately preceding the opening parenthesis should be placed after the closing parenthesis: 76

Thomas (his old schoolfellow) was just entering the room.

He caught sight of Thomas (his old schoolfellow), whom now he scarcely recognized.

The features were clearly those of Thomas (his old schoolfellow): the same high cheekbones, the humorous eyes, the sensitive mouth.

8 BRACKETS

Brackets, as distinct from parentheses, are square-cornered. 77

Brackets are used to indicate a comment or an explanation inserted by someone other than the author of the text in which they occur: 78

'It was not for me', said Johnson, 'to bandy civilities with my Sovereign [George III].'

Note that the final bracket is set before the full point and final quote.

The following would be **wrong:**

. . . with my Sovereign.' [George III]
. . . with my Sovereign' [George III].

79 Brackets may similarly be used in reported speech:

Dr Johnson said that it was not for him to bandy civilities with his Sovereign [George III].

80 Brackets are also useful for enclosing parenthetical matter in a sentence that is already enclosed in parentheses:

Malvolio (the reference to whom as 'a kind of puritan' [*Twelfth Night* II, iii, 137] sufficiently indicates his temperament) is always represented as soberly clad.

9 EXCLAMATION MARK

81 When a word of exclamation is repeated, the exclamation mark is placed only after the last word, each of the other words being followed by a comma:

Ha, ha, ha!   **not:** Ha! Ha! Ha!

82 The mark of exclamation, though it includes a full point, is not necessarily followed by a capital letter:

Excellent! you've done really well.

83 An exclamation mark may be inserted by the author in parentheses, to indicate astonishment or incredulity:

He said he really loved (!) being ill.

84 If inserted in brackets, it indicates the same feeling on the part of the editor:

After weeks of such frightful boredom, danger was a positive relief [!].

If an exclamation mark follows immediately upon a word in italic, it should not be set likewise in italic unless it belongs strictly to the italicized word preceding it: 85

You cut the bread now; but for heaven's sake, not so *thick*!
not: *thick!*

The fellow turned up at his own wedding wearing a yellow *béret*!
not: *béret!*

but: Oh, *help!* **not:** Oh, *help*!

10 QUESTION MARK

An indirect question should not be followed by a note of interrogation: 86

He wondered if she would ever stop talking.
not: . . . if she would ever stop talking?

but contrast the following:

He wondered, would she ever stop talking?

A sentence cast in the form of a question does not invariably require a question mark: 87

Will you please stop talking.

May I offer you my congratulations.

'How d'you do', he said.

And at that moment whom should he see on the opposite pavement but the very man who had brought about his disgrace.

As I got out of the train, whom did I recognize but Alan himself.

Conversely, in quoted dialogue, a question mark may conclude a sentence which in form is not strictly a question: 88

Surely you aren't going to that length?

Supposing that there is no after-life?

A question may sometimes require not a question mark but a note of exclamation: 89

Well now, I ask you! How stupid can you be!

Won't someone give me a hand!

How awful! What ever did you feel like!

Shut up, man! Will you shut up!

I say, aren't the children having fun!

After all, what is life but a hideous joke!

Stop the cab, will you!

Isn't it lovely to see them all again!

90 A question mark inserted in parentheses indicates doubt on the part of the author of the truth of the statement he is making:

He has no doubts whatever (?) on reincarnation.

91 If the question mark is placed in brackets, on the other hand, it expresses scepticism on the part of the editor:

He declared, 'You know, I actually enjoy [?] thunderstorms.'

92 If a question mark follows immediately upon a word in italic, it is not to be set likewise in italic unless it belongs strictly to the italicized word preceding it:

Have you read *The Last Days of Pompeii*? **not:** *Pompeii?*

I dare say you know that Bulwer-Lytton also wrote a book entitled *What Will He Do with It?*

11 APOSTROPHE

93 Singular nouns ending in *s* should take *'s* in the possessive case:

St James's Street	*but:* St James' Club
Inigo Jones's art	*Pears Cyclopaedia*
Cecil Rhodes's career	
Dickens's novels	
Graves's disease	

Keats's poems
Brooks's Club
the jackass's laughter
the octopus's tentacles
the rhinoceros's horn

A reminder must be given that possessive pronouns do not take an apostrophe: ***her's, our's, their's, your's*** are all **wrong**; ***it's*** is not the possessive pronoun, but a contraction for *it is*; the possessive pronoun is *its*. 94

Nouns ending in *s* normally take *es* in the plural: 95

keeping up with the Joneses	**not:**	with the Jones'
	nor:	with the Jones's

but in the plural possessive case they take only the apostrophe without a further *s*:

We called at the Joneses' house.
I was staying at the Joneses'.

But note that *'s* is used in plurals of some single letters: 96

dot the i's and cross the t's
mind your p's and q's **not:** '*p*'s and '*q*'s

Note that '*ps* and *qs*' is practicable only if the roman 's' of the fount does not dwarf the italic letters.

The apostrophe does not properly belong to the plural form, and should not be printed unless necessary for clarity: 97

during the 1920s	**not:** 1920's
the three Rs	**not:** R's
a number of M.P.s	**not:** M.P.'s **nor:** M.P's **nor:** M.Ps

Note this usage, which is inconsistent but correct: 98

all these do's and dont's

The apostrophe preceding the *s* is introduced to clarify what might otherwise be an unintelligible plural form: 99

The frequent set-to's were usually of her making.

In speaking he's always confusing I's and me's.

We must weigh carefully the pro's and con's.

The London operatic stage has seen several *Rigoletto*'s recently.

I like his broad north-country speech with its 'thou's' and 'thee's'.

100 The apostrophe is also used to indicate the omission of part of a word:

She had done her training as a physio'. (i.e. physiotherapist)

That morning, strange to say, the pro's were no match for the amateurs.

101 Note also the following correct forms, in which an apostrophe might have been expected:

St Albans
St Andrews
St Bees
St Davids, Fifeshire *but:* St David's, Pembrokeshire
St Helens
St Ives
St Leonards
St Neots, Huntingdonshire *but:* St Neot, Cornwall

102 Following the example of London Transport, it has become increasingly common to print Earls Court, St Pauls, etc. without the apostrophe.
Note also:

Lloyds Bank Harrods Palmers Green Shepherds Bush

103 Print apostrophe without *s* where the possessive *s* is not pronounced:

for clearness' sake
for conscience' sake
for convenience' sake

for goodness' sake *but:* for heaven's sake
interference for interference' sake
He said it just for politeness' sake.

and also in singular forms of classical and biblical names: 104

Zeus' thunderbolts
Sophocles' tragedies
Moses' law
for Jesus' sake Note often in hymns: Jesu's

and also where pronunciation is especially difficult: 105

the Mercedes' exhaust
Barbara Villiers' intrigues
Gezelle was one of Flanders' greatest poets.

French proper names ending in *s* or *x* should be followed by 106
's in the possessive case:

Louis's
Delacroix's

Note *The Beaux' Stratagem*; but do not imitate this precedent in other uses of this French word.

'd (formerly *'ld*) is a contraction for *would*. 107
d' is an abbreviation for *do*.

How 'd you . . . ? = How would you . . . ?
How d'you . . . ? = How do you . . . ?
If I were to say nothing, how 'd you know what I was thinking?
If I never answer, how d'you know what I'm thinking?
How 'd you have known if he hadn't told you?

'd, *'ed*, may also be used to create an adjective either from 108
a noun or from a verb, at the writer's own fancy:

a one-idea'd eccentric
a well précis'd memorandum

His socks were concertina'ed round his ankles.

He hum'd and ha'd a good deal before making up his mind.

109 Before a shortened numeral (whether spelt out or not) indicating a decade of years, the apostrophe should be printed to mark the omission of the century:

the '20s

the hungry 'forties (= 1840s)

but: the roaring forties (= 40° S. latitude)

the 'Fifteen and the 'Forty-five

but of course not where the reference is only to the decade of a man's life:

There is a portrait of him in the thirties. (i.e. in his thirties)

110 Note that 'teens', 'teenagers', etc. now have no apostrophe. Nor have the following:

bus flu phone plane

12 HYPHEN

111 There are few logical rules on hyphenation. Certain practical rulings are therefore all the more important. CHAMBERS tends to overdo hyphenation and should not be followed uncritically. American usage, on the other hand, is too sparing in the use of hyphens for contemporary English taste; readers do not at present take kindly to such forms as *absentmindedly*, *makebelieve*, *makeup*, *makeweight*, *manchild*, *muddleheaded*, *shareout*, *takeover*. But English taste shows signs of moving away from hyphens.

112 Hyphenate compound adjectives of various types:

(a) adjectives formed from an adjective followed by a noun:

the next-door house *but:* the house next door

the old-age pension(er)

a worth-while journey *but:* The journey was worth while.

The luncheon was dreadfully third-rate.

an effective central-heating system

a one-time champion

a slow-motion process

It seemed slow-motion by comparison.

a full-face portrait

(b) adjectives formed from a noun followed by an adjective: 113

The colour was sea-green.

It was a blood-red sunset over the wine-dark ocean.

He had a bird-like nose and was ankle-deep in mud.

She was wearing a very effective mustard-yellow ensemble.

How well an emerald-green scarf goes with ginger-red hair!

There are three traffic lights: danger-red, amber-yellow and safety-green.

(c) adjectives formed from a present participle, preceded by an adjective or adverb: 114

good-looking long-lasting hard-wearing easy-going
never-ending never-failing (but note: backsliding)

He had an unlikely-sounding name for an Englishman.

The whole scheme was remarkably forward-looking.

(d) adjectives formed from a past participle qualified by an adverb: 115

a well-kept garden *but:* The garden was well kept.

an ill-informed fellow *but:* The fellow was ill informed.

The above-mentioned members have not yet paid their subscriptions this year.

but: The members above mentioned will be struck off the roll.

His so-called bravery was, in fact, fear of public opinion.

but: his bravery, so called by comparison with the abject cowardice of the others

Several grown-ups were present. *but:* By this time he was grown up.

a long-drawn-out affair *but:* The trial was long drawn out.

the widest-spread and longest-lasting of Man's conceptions

116 Beware of inserting hyphens where they are unnecessary:

The enemy had been fought off. **not:** fought-off

a roughly sketched picture **not:** roughly-sketched

a beautifully furnished room **not:** beautifully-furnished

Note the difference between:

more closely packed cells

and:

more closely-packed cells

117 (e) adjectives formed from a verb and a preposition, perhaps with an adverb preceding them:

His success in the exam had been quite unhoped-for.

No matter how strongly he spoke, his advice was unlistened-to.

They all looked thoroughly well-cared-for.

118 (f) adjectives formed from an adverbial phrase:

a near-by stream *but:* the stream near by

an all-out effort *but:* He went all out for his great objective.

He used up-to-date methods, but his information was never up to date.

119 (g) adjectives formed from two adjectives:

the dark-blue sea a light-green coat He was ashen-pale.

120 (h) adjectives formed from a past participle preceded by a noun:

She was a convent-educated type.

his American-born wife

a Glasgow-born docker

the Nazi-occupied section of the country

Distinguish between:

the English-occupied town of Calais

and:

the French occupied town of Calais

(i) adjectives made up of a phrase of two or more words: **121**

his matter-of-fact style

a penny-a-week fund

a rough-and-ready manner

I'm afraid we're among the not-so-wealthy.

Everything was looking really spick-and-span.

a cell-to-cell movement

He was at once on the scene, with his civil-servant's sense of duty.

The Negro looked unusual with his white-man's haircut.

in the common-or-garden meaning of the term

his never-to-be-forgotten kindness

The thingummy-bob – you know, the what-d'ye-call-it.

Hyphenate certain compound nouns: **122**

(a) nouns formed from a verb, or verbal noun, and an adverb or adjective:

There's no doubt they have all the know-how.

Am I to take this critical step simply on your say-so?

a shake-down   a take-over   a shake-up   a lean-to

the be-all and end-all of the whole business

I tell you, there was a pretty sizeable to-do over it all.

He's a has-been.

It's just part of his make-up.

There was the usual crowd of hangers-on.

He was a great diner-out.

I tell you, it's all pure make-believe.

123 (b) nouns formed from a noun and a verbal phrase appended to it:

the bride-to-be

In the conventionally dressed young man before him there was not a trace of the beatnik-that-was.

124 (c) nouns formed from two nouns, the former being in the possessive case:

a bob's-worth of sweets three shillings'-worth of sausages

There, within arm's-length, stood the man he had sworn to track down.

A stone's-throw? why, it wasn't more than half a stone's-throw!

crane's-bill

death's-head

lamb's-wool

neat's-foot oil *but:* calves-foot jelly

no-man's-land

125 Hyphenate nouns and adjectives compounded with *near-*:

That was a near-miss.

He suffered near-martyrdom.

It was a tricky situation: the men were near-mutinous.

Even in his death agony, a near-smile came to his lips.

126 Note the contrast between the presence and absence of the hyphen in the following:

He had a deeply felt and ever-increasing awareness of . . .
They were a highly sensitive newly-married couple.

He found him in high spirits.
Throughout the evening he was in the most violent high-spirits.

They saw that the boy was well-educated.
They saw to it that the boy was well educated.

The sanitation of the farm was shocking: the cows were drinking near-sewage. **not:** The cows were drinking near sewage.

Hyphenate adjectives or adverbs formed from nouns or adjectives compounded with *-fashion*, *-style*, *-type*, *-size*, etc. 127

She was wearing a 1920-style cloche hat.

They had scarves on their heads coif-fashion.

a tycoon-size cigar

a Kikuyu-language newspaper

his clerical-type charcoal-grey suit

but: all cleaned up and Bristol fashion

Hyphenate numbers compounded: 128

(a) with adjectives:

a crowd of fifty-odd people

230-odd people **not:** two hundred and thirty-odd people

the 150,000-strong Civil Service Clerical Association

(b) with nouns denoting a measure of time or space: 129

a six-foot ladder a 100-yard-long lawn

a fifteen-year lease

a 150-year period of growth

a 25-year-old man **not:** a twenty-five-year-old man

but: a six months' sentence

a five years' term

a nine minutes' start

In three-word expressions, take care that the hyphen is in the right place: 130

wild-goose chase	**not:** wild goose-chase
waste-paper basket	**not:** waste paper-basket
hot-water bottle	**not:** hot water-bottle
fine-tooth comb	**not:** fine tooth-comb
small-tooth comb	**not:** small tooth-comb
brown-paper parcel	**not:** brown paper-parcel
cod-liver oil	**not:** cod liver-oil
low-water mark	**not:** low water-mark

Contrast for meaning:

ritual-murder trials	ritual murder-trials
rare-book collector	rare book-collector

131 Hyphenate to distinguish a difference in meaning:

re-bound	rebound	re-enforce	reinforce
re-count	recount	re-form	reform
re-cover	recover	re-join	rejoin
re-dress	redress	re-press	repress

132 Hyphenate when two identical letters are adjacent but belong to different syllables and are pronounced separately:

beach-hut	head-dress	re-entry
co-ordinate	Inverness-shire	Ross-shire
dumb-bell	Kinross-shire	shirt-tail
eel-like	news-stand	ski-ing
glow-worm	pre-eminent	Tees-side
grand-daughter	re-enable	watch-chain

but: Dumfriesshire withhold

133 Hyphenate when a lower-case prefix has to be separated from an initial capital letter:

pre-Christian pro-French un-English to out-Herod Herod

134 Hyphenate when a suffix, such as *-ish*, *-ite*, is appended to a surname preceded by a first name or title:

He had a Samuel Smiles-ish conception of 'self-help'.

The Oswald Mosley-ites turned up in force.

He was an enthusiastic Major Douglas-ite.

On the other hand,

Benthamite Hitlerite Russellite

have no hyphen.

When two or more hyphenated words have one part in common, the variable part should be followed or preceded by the hyphen and a space: 135

the third- and fourth-century styles

the eighteenth- and early-nineteenth-century classicists

fifty-five or -six years of age

He was a much younger man . . . about twenty-six or -seven.

The Spanish rock-paintings and -engravings fall into three main groups.

Breuil was indefatigable on horse- or mule-back.

His long life makes it possible to see him against both a nineteenth- and a twentieth-century background.

both his sister- and brother-in-law

It was on either Twenty-second or -third Street.

Hyphenate French place names that include *Saint*(*e*): 136

Saint-Jean-de-Luz   Sainte-Menehould   Mont-Saint-Michel

but not usually outside France:

Saint Georges (French Guiana)   Sainte Rose (Quebec)

Surnames are of course often hyphenated: 137

Bulwer-Lytton   Quiller-Couch   Toulouse-Lautrec
Plunkett-Ernle-Erle-Drax   Twisleton-Wykeham-Fiennes
Vane-Tempest-Stewart   von Wilamowitz-Moellendorf

It is also important to note surnames which consist of more than one word and are not hyphenated: 138

Bruce Lockhart   Lloyd George   Vaughan Williams

and others which are sometimes hyphenated, sometimes not: 139

Bonham Carter   Clifton Brown

French Christian names are often hyphenated: 140

Jean-Jacques Rousseau   Jean-Paul Sartre

141 But do not hyphenate English surnames or titles beginning with *Saint*:

St Aldwyn St Barbe St Clair St Denys St George
St John St Leger St Quinton St Ruth St Vincent

142 Note, however, the French surnames:

Saint-Denis St-Cyr

143 Hyphenate expressions of time and decades of years:

during the eighteen-nineties
I missed the six-fifteen train but managed to catch the six-thirty.

144 Hyphenate when the conjunction of two words unhyphenated would produce a single compound letter form:

wolf-like **not:** wolflike
cuff-links **not:** cufflinks
self-inflicted wounds **not:** selfinflicted wounds

145 Spelt-out fractions are to be hyphenated:

one-sixth two-thirds three-quarters five-sixteenths
in the two-and-a-half years since he had left

but note that in some such expressions the hyphen is not to be used:

a whole half-hour *but:* half an hour **not:** half-an-hour
for the next quarter-hour
I'll call for you at half past; we can talk on the way to the station, and you'll catch the train at a quarter to.
They won by a half-length. a three-quarter-length sleeve

146 *half* sometimes demands a hyphen, but is often as well without it:

a half-demented wretch
These people are half savages.
She saw the door was half open.
She approached the half-open door.

The beach was half covered with shingle.

He was already half-drunk or, as the phrase goes, half seas over.

His tone was half serious, half mocking.

I groped forward, half-blinded by the fog.

'What in heaven's name has happened?' he cried, half mad with anxiety.

She rose in annoyance at his presumption, and there he was left, half kneeling in front of the coal scuttle. As he picked himself up, the expression on his face was half rueful, half genuinely amused.

The old fellow was talking half under his breath and could scarcely be heard.

'Oh dear, is it time to get up already?' he grumbled, half opening his eyes.

The sunlight was pouring into the room, but his eyes were only half-open.

Though she was sitting next to him at table, she remained throughout the meal with her shoulder half turned away from him.

Even when she was speaking to him, her half-turned shoulder seemed to show a deliberate coolness on her part.

fellow should be joined to the following word by a hyphen in the most commonly used instances: **147**

fellow-man fellow-citizen fellow-countryman

fellow-feeling fellow-soldier fellow-traveller

But with less common forms, the hyphen is not to be regarded as obligatory. With longish words, or two-word phrases, it is usually better omitted, so long as there is no glaring inconsistency with other words on the same page: **148**

He was on good terms with his fellow scientists.

I was delighted to come across a fellow Englishman so far from home.

his fellow Cabinet Ministers a fellow propagandist

Protestant and Catholic are, after all, fellow Christians.

149 The following examples will illustrate the two-way direction of English taste in hyphens:

	parlourmaid	**not:** parlour-maid
but:	under-parlourmaid	**not:** underparlourmaid
	clockwise	**not:** clock-wise
but:	anti-clockwise	**not:** anticlockwise

150 The desirable end of reducing the number of hyphens may be achieved:

(a) by joining the two words:

uphill downhill upstream downstream sidesaddle

But this must be done with discretion, if offence is not to be given to English taste.

151 (b) by keeping the two words quite separate:

You can gain entrance through the side door.

But that is purely a side issue; please stick to the main point.

He nipped smartly down a side street, and vanished completely.

He was of a High Church persuasion.

Evangelicals are by no means necessarily Low Churchmen.

The talks were shortly brought out in book form.

I shouldn't like to judge this at its face value.

152 Contrast for usage:

chicken pox scrum-pox smallpox

153 Hyphenation must ultimately be a matter of discretion. Consistency is of prime importance.

The following lists may serve as guides to discretion whether to separate or join words rather than hyphenate:

armchair	candlestick	breast pocket
backbiting	chessboard	case history
bookseller	clockwise	common sense

daydream	muckraking	death warrant
eardrums	newspaperman	drawing room
endpapers	notebook	drinking party
footbrake	pacemaker	fir tree
handlebar	peacemaker	good looks
highlight	peacetime	ill health
horsepower	piecemeal	man hours
innsign	plainchant	market town
lamplighter	shakedown	motor car
landmark	sidewalk	motor cycle
landowner	slapdash	music hall
lawgiver	spearhead	neap tide
lawsuit	springtime	nettle rash
layby	stateroom	no one
layout	stockbroker	nose dive
limestone	summertime	period piece
livestock	teacup	price list
maidservant	textbook	reading lamp
manpower	tortoiseshell	side gate
manservant	wartime	side turning
midday	watermark	source book
midway	waterworks	tea leaves
midwinter	wrongdoing	wrist watch

13 QUOTES

Single quotes should normally be used; double quotes within; and, if necessary, further single quotes within double. 154

> 'Let us take the matter a little further', said counsel. 'A few moments ago you used these words: "I saw the accused warning the witness to keep out of this case." That is so, isn't it?' — 'Yes, that's what I said.'

'Now, I put it to you: did you really mean "saw"?' — 'I don't understand you.'
'Well, sir: are you telling the Court that it was clear to you from the accused's *actions*, quite apart from any *words* he may or may not have uttered, that he was giving the witness this warning?' — 'I don't know what you mean; I saw him talking to the witness.'
'But that didn't tell you what he was saying. Do you mean to say that you "saw" some threatening gestures on his part?' — 'No, I didn't say that.'
'Then, perhaps you didn't mean "saw"? What you really meant was "heard"?' — 'Well, yes, I suppose it was.'

155 Quotes are required for colloquial terms, or where single words or phrases are referred to:

He was a proper 'cockney sparrer'.

The word 'expert' may well intimidate the amateur.

It was organized on a 'first come, first served' basis.

'But you said No', he repeated. 'What did that "No" mean?'

156 Unspoken dialogue or thoughts may be left without quotes, unless there is some special reason for inserting them:

Now what are they thinking? I asked myself.

Awkward fellows, he thought; they're always up to something or other.

157 Punctuation which is part of the quoted phrase or sentence should be set within the quotes:

'Had I heard,' he said, 'I should have answered.'

[What he actually said was: 'Had I heard, I should have answered.']

'Don't worry,' she said, 'you shall have my things all in good time' (i.e. after her death).

[Her words were: 'Don't worry, you shall have my things . . .']

Note that when the final full point of the quoted matter coincides with the end of the sentence, the full point should be set within the final quote.

Punctuation which is not part of the original sentence is to be set outside the quotes: 158

He described the fellow's suggestion as 'not far short of blackmail'.

'To resist it', he urged, 'demands the utmost courage.'

[He said: 'To resist it demands the utmost courage.']

'Dr B.', she wrote, 'knows nothing more about it than the other doctors.'

[**not:** 'Dr B.,' she wrote, 'knows nothing . . . ' for she did not write: 'Dr B., knows nothing . . . ']

'Now, you must take this drink "as hot as you can bear it", as the doctor said.'

His most popular picture, 'The Monarch of the Glen', decorates to this day scores upon scores of front parlours at seaside towns.

The whole design was vitiated by what were intended as 'artistic effects'.

'And how fussy he was! He said he must have everything "just right".'

'The Oxford or Cambridge M.A.', he maintained, 'adds no further distinction to the B.A. already conferred by the university.'

but: 'The Oxford or Cambridge M.A.,' he maintained, 'unlike that of Durham and other universities, adds no further distinction to the . . . '

He wrote in his diary: 'I have never been at work on so many projects at a time', following this note with a list of eleven scripts which were then absorbing his attention.

'I often call to mind the words: "Blessed are the peacemakers" ', he said.

but: He replied: 'I often call to mind the words: "Blessed are the peacemakers." '

'But what', I broke in, 'did he say about the accident?'

'What difference', he used to ask, 'can it possibly make?'

'It was', he said, 'the worst thing that could have happened.'

[**wrong:** 'It was,' he said, 'the worst thing that could have happened'.]

He described it as 'the worst thing that could have happened'.

[**wrong:** He described it as 'the worst thing that could have happened.']

Calling them all 'filthy swine', he turned on his heel and stamped out.

'Brother Charles,' said Wesley, 'you and I have much still to do.'

'Brother Charles', said Wesley, 'writes good hymns', and not a word more would he say.

159 In the following sentence no comma is needed:

'Egypt for the Egyptians' was the only cry the mob understood.

160 If the quotation extends to more than one paragraph, each subsequent paragraph must start with a quote, but only the final paragraph will end with a quote.

14 QUOTED MATTER

161 Quoted matter in prose, if it exceeds five lines of copy, should be broken off from the text, set in type one size smaller, indented one em, without quotes. The first line should be full out.

162 Broken-off quoted matter is not necessarily followed by a new paragraph in the text. Unless a new paragraph is indicated in copy, the line of text following the quoted matter should be full out.

A few lines will give some idea of what she wrote:

> The police superintendent took some paper and told me to describe to him what had happened at the grotto. I did so. After writing down some lines as I had dictated them, he put down other things that I had never heard of....

Throughout the remaining twenty-one years of her life she stood by every detail of the account she had then given, despite all efforts to shake her testimony to these remarkable happenings.

A brief sentence interpolated into the quoted matter by way of introduction may be set in the broken-off matter within brackets: 163

> The company gradually settled in their seats and the guest of honour stood up to speak.
>
> > Had I known [he said with emotion] that I was to meet so many of my friends tonight, and perhaps for the last time before I leave for a journey which will keep me out of this country for many years, I would have considered more carefully than I have in fact had time to do, how to make the best use of these few moments I have in which to talk to you.
>
> He paused briefly, and there was sympathetic applause from his audience.

Quoted matter is often introduced by a colon after the word immediately preceding, but this is not always correct. The following, for example, is **wrong**: 164

> As has often been said: 'Too many cooks spoil the broth.'

The following are correct:

> As has often been said, 'Too many cooks spoil the broth.'
>
> As Aristotle long ago declared, 'Man is a political animal.'

The guiding rule is to adopt normal punctuation in leading into a passage of quoted matter: 165

> One who knew him well has written that in his youth
>
> > he was most approachable, kind to everyone he met, and especially sympathetic to those in trouble; . . .

Sometimes the quoted matter may be introduced by a phrase leading directly into its first sentence, which should then be preceded by an ellipsis: 166

> In this city there is to be found, he writes,
>
> > . . . such a profusion of fascinating buildings of the Renaissance and later periods that one could spend months in the study of them and even then not have exhausted all the delights which this charming region has to offer.

167 Quoted matter in verse, even of only one line, should be similarly broken off from the text, set in smaller type, indented and without quotes unless the lines of poetry are spoken.

168 It may be introduced as variously as quoted matter in prose. The following passages will illustrate:

> There are two famous sayings of Satan in *Paradise Lost*. One is:
>
> > Which way I fly is hell; myself am hell;
>
> the other is:
>
> > The mind is its own place, and in itself
> > Can make a heaven of hell, a hell of heaven.
>
> When Raphael comes down to instruct Adam, we are told that
>
> > at the gate
> > Of Heaven arrived, the gate self-opened wide
> > On golden hinges turning.
>
> Again, as Raphael explains to Adam,
>
> > We also have our evening and our morn,
> > We ours for change delectable, not need.

169 Quotes are of course to be used in quoted matter within verse:

> 'Awake, arise, or be for ever fall'n!'
> They heard, and were abashed, and up they sprung
> Upon the wing, . . .

15 CAPITALS AND SMALL CAPITALS

170 In general avoid capitals wherever possible. A page clogged with caps does not present a dignified appearance. In such books as academic chronicles or regimental histories it may be difficult to thin out the degrees, ranks and decorations, but here relief may be found in the use of small caps.

Distinguish a particular from a general meaning: 171

Long live the King!	A cat may look at a king.
the Bible	Wisden is the cricket-lover's bible.
off to the Continent	throughout the continent of Europe
I think Father is right.	I believe in my father.
the Communist Party	He had communist leanings.
the Book of Revelation	all the books of Holy Scripture

Degrees, decorations, honours and titles of distinction after proper names should be set in small caps; but in caps if they stand alone: 172

John Smith M.A.	*but:* He is working on his Ph.D. thesis.
Robert Jones G.M.	*but:* Never was the G.M. more thoroughly deserved.
Richard James D.S.O.	*but:* He won the D.S.O. for gallantry in 1917.
Thomas Huxley F.R.S.	*but:* The F.R.S. is one of the highest distinctions.

A.D. and B.C., whether standing alone or as part of a date, should normally be set thus, in small capitals: 173

Throughout the fourth century A.D., the barbarians continued to pour into Italy.

There is no starting point for the years B.C.

Do not capitalize the following titles of address, when used alone: 174

sir	mister	my lord	monsieur
madam	missus	my lady	mademoiselle
mamma	miss	m'lud	monsignor
master			papa

175 but at the beginning of a letter, or when the name follows, capitalize:

 My dear Sir Dear Madam

 Master Ridley Miss Austen

 Sir Walter Ralegh Madame Tussaud

176 Note the following distinction:

 His Majesty their Highnesses

 Your Grace their Majesties

177 Hyphenated titles are to be capitalized in both parts:

 Major-General Vice-President Sub-Dean

 Paymaster-General

178 The Deity should always be capitalized in exclamations and in compound words where serious reference is intended:

 Good God! He was a God-fearing man.

 But, my God, what on earth have you done?

179 but not capitalized where there is no explicit or serious reference:

 good lord! What a god-forsaken hole!

 this godless generation Curse these goddam flies!

 Why, lord knows what he'll do next!

 But, lawks ha' mercy, did yer ever see the like!

 . . . and, my dear, you can't imagine, it was an absolute godsend.

180 Distinguish between:

 Do tell me, darling, who *is* that absolutely godlike young man?

and:

 The human reason has a God-like capacity.

Personal pronouns referring to the Deity or to any Person of the Christian Trinity are often, but by no means invariably, capitalized. Capitalization was the general rule in the nineteenth century, though not earlier. It is noteworthy that the Authorized and other received Versions of the Bible do not capitalize, and modern usage is tending to revert to this earlier tradition. Certainly no question of reverence is involved. **181**

Relative pronouns referring to the Deity are in no case to be capitalized. **182**

Capitalize the following: **183**

Negro Aborigine (Abo)

Political and geographical divisions should be capitalized, but not the points of the compass when printed in full: **184**

the Near East	east of the Pennines
South-East Asia	south-east Durham
German South-West Africa	a south-west wind
Northern Ireland	the whole of northern England
the Middle East	to the north-east
the Western Hemisphere	down to the west country

Seasons of the year are not to be capitalized: **185**

Don't you think autumn is in some ways the loveliest time of the year?

Off to the Bahamas, old boy? What! taking your summer holiday in the middle of the winter? Good idea!

It may sometimes, however, be necessary to capitalize *Spring* to avoid ambiguity: **186**

For a time after Christmas the watch worked perfectly; it was the spring that showed its unreliability. No, I don't mean the watch-spring; I mean the Spring: spring of the year, and all that, don'tcher know!

187 Note that American addresses are to be capitalized thus:

He had moved up to West Fifty-ninth Street.
Their house is on either Twenty-sixth or -seventh.

188 Capitalize 'yes' and 'no' when treated as nouns:

What I want from you is a plain Yes or No.
A child must learn to accept a No.

189 The following are instances of capitalization for the sake of clarity:

	but:
the (Royal) Academy	
an Act (of Parliament)	
the Bank (of England)	my bank manager
the Bench (of judges)	the bench of bishops
	the Treasury bench
	a bench-warrant
a (Parliamentary) Bill	a bill of attainder
	a bill of complaint
	a bill of exchange
the Cabinet	a cabinet minister
the (Roman Catholic, Methodist) Church	a (parish, cathedral) church
the City (of London)	
the Forces	the (land, sea and air) forces of the Crown
the Government (as a semi-personal body)	under government control
the House (of Commons, of Lords)	
the Member (of Parliament) for . . .	
the Minister, Ministry (of State)	a minister of religion

the Press	a press proof
the Services	the armed services
the State (secular government)	the state of Louisiana, state papers
the States (-General)	
Covent Garden Opera House	Covent Garden is the national opera house.
The Court made an order.	The court was cleared.

She sought the Court's protection.

He took the firm to court and sued them.

The Lyric Theatre is on the left of Shaftesbury Avenue.

He was a prominent figure in the Left theatre.

She quickly made her name in the theatre of the 'nineties.

It was a matter of church government rather than of state administration.

The relations between Church and State had undergone profound change.

When the name of an institution is repeated in a shorter form, the initial capital letter should be retained: **190**

At a meeting of the A.A. it was unanimously decided that the Association should make representations to the authorities.

Astronomical and geological names should be capitalized throughout: **191**

the Great Bear	Orion's Belt
Charles's Wain	the Upper Pleistocene

but in Latin names of animals, plants, etc. the first word only should have an initial cap (even though the second word may indicate a proper name): **192**

Pithecanthropus erectus	*Galeocerdo cuvier*
Nigella damascena	*Isistius brasiliensis*
Passer domesticus	*Viola tricolor*

193 Certain words in common use may be found to be proprietary names or registered trade-names which the firm concerned may require to be capitalized. Examples are:

Land-Rover Spam Terylene Thermos Vaseline

194 The initial letters of some adjectives and nouns derived from places, peoples or individual persons are, in certain connexions, now commonly set in lower case. Examples are:

arabic or roman (numerals)
asian (flu)
balkanization
bohemian
china tea
chinese white
draconian measures
french leave
french polish
french windows
herculean struggle
holland material
homeric laughter
italic or roman (type)
morocco leather
philippic
plaster of paris
platonic friendship
prussian blue
quisling
russia leather
satanic
scotch and soda
sisyphean task
socratic irony
trilby hat
turkey carpet
turkey red
turkish bath
venetian blinds
virginia creeper
wellingtons

195 Titles of books, periodicals, articles, literary, musical and artistic works, names of theatres and public buildings should have initial capital letters, except for the word *and*, the definite and indefinite articles, and prepositions making up the title.

The Last Days of Pompeii

'Ode on Intimations of Immortality'

the Duke of York's Theatre

'Sohrab and Rustum'

'The Wreck of the Hesperus'

Journal of a Disappointed Man

French, Spanish and Italian titles capitalize the first word, and the second word also if the first is an article. An adjective preceding and qualifying a capitalized noun also takes a capital letter. The rest of the title is lower case, except for proper nouns. 196

German titles capitalize the first word and all nouns.

English titles of foreign works, if following the title in the original language, should be set in upper and lower case roman within quotes.

La Russie et l'église universelle ('Russia and the Universal Church')

Del Sentimiento trágico de la vida ('The Tragic Sense of Life')

I Promessi Sposi ('The Betrothed')

Le Travail en miettes ('The Anatomy of Work')

Im Westen Nichts Neues ('All Quiet on the Western Front')

If the English translation has itself been published, its title should be given in its published form.

16 FIGURES

In ordinary descriptive or narrative prose, avoid setting figures at the beginning of a sentence following a previous full point; the author may sometimes meet this difficulty by replacing the preceding full point by a semicolon. In works which contain much statistical material, it may frequently be necessary to begin a sentence with figures; care should then be taken to choose a type face which includes lining figures commensurate in dignity with the capitals of the same face. 197

198 Non-lining figures are usually preferable to lining figures. But both are not always available in the same fount.

199 Lining figures may in any case be preferable:
(i) in tabular matter
(ii) in works in which figures are frequently associated with caps:

the A30 road *rather than:* the A30 road

(iii) in works containing many figures: dates, mathematical statistics, etc. It may often be impossible to avoid setting these at the beginning of sentences. Non-lining figures may be dwarfed by caps of the same fount and will therefore look disproportionate and undignified at the beginning of a sentence.

1962 had been a prosperous year. 20,000 bushels of wheat alone were exported in the twelve months. 1963, however, saw a marked decline in production.

200 Non-lining figures are more suitable with small caps: S.W.15

201 Non-lining figures are also more appropriate with small caps in headlines.

202 Numbers under 100 should normally be spelt out.

By noon about eighty-four people had turned up.

203 Numbers of 100 and over should be expressed in figures.

The average attendance last year was at least 150.

204 But if a number under 100 is associated with a number of 100 or over, use figures for both numbers.

Of every 100 children born only 24 lived as long as a year.

205 If, however, numbers of 100 or over denote a vague, rather than an exact, quantity, they should be spelt out:

I had a hundred and one things to do that day.

Forty million Frenchmen can't be wrong.

this magnificent thousand-year-old mausoleum

To express round numbers in millions, with no stress on the exact sum, use figures coupled with the word 'million' in the singular: 206

£24 million   or: £24m.   [**not:** £24 millions   **nor:** £24,000,000]
153 million miles
Out of a 12-million electorate only 4 million voted.

but for a series of precise quantities – measurements, percentages, ages, statistics of various kinds – use figures: 207

5 per cent
29 ft long and only 2 in. thick
They were respectively 18, 25, and 42 years old.
His temperature was a little over 99.

When a single age is given, not in comparison with others, spell it out: 208

The boy was fourteen last birthday.

Do not combine an already hyphenated number with other hyphenated words. In this case, express the number in figures, even if it is under 100: 209

She also had a 73-year-old husband to look after.
not: seventy-three-year-old

Spell out numbers enumerating centuries, unless two or more centuries are mentioned together: 210

eighteenth-century culture
but: during the 12th–13th-century growth of political stability

In sequences of numbers, as a general rule, use the least number of figures possible; that is to say, do not normally repeat the tens figure: 211

pp. 387–9   **not:** pp. 387–89

but the figure 1 in teens must always be repeated: 212

pp. 214–16   **not:** pp. 214–6

213 Two exceptions to this rule should be noted: In phrases expressing extent of days of the month (see **231**) and of verses of Scripture (see **399**), the tens figure should always be repeated.

214 When roman numerals are used to express extent of numbers, the full figures must of course be given:

pp. xxvii–xxviii

pp. ci–ciii

215 Note that the en rule, **not** the hyphen, is to be used to mark extent of numbers.

216 Use figures for the time of day, when combined with the abbreviations 'a.m.', 'p.m.' Otherwise spell out the number:

He began work at 8.30 a.m. and did not leave his desk until twenty to six.

The time is now two o'clock: you will be able to catch the three-thirty easily and you will be in London shortly after five.

217 In decimal numbers, use decimal (raised) points normally; but in decimal coinage – dollars, francs, deutschmarks, etc. – use full points on the line:

10·85 *but:* \$10.85 NF 6.25 DM 8.30

218 A decimal number less than 1 requires a cipher before the decimal point:

0·43 **not:** ·43

219 Fractions between 1 and 2 take a plural noun and verb:

1 yard was not enough but 1½ yards have usually been adequate.

About 1¾ hours were reckoned as time spent on the job.

220 In numbers consisting of four or more figures a comma is to be inserted before every three:

2,379,606

But note that no comma should be inserted in the following:

(i) numbers of verse lines:	*Paradise Lost* ii, 1021
(ii) library and MS. numbers:	Add. MS. 34852
(iii) year numbers:	A.D. 1066
(iv) page numbers:	p. 1146
(v) telephone numbers:	788 9573
(vi) early car-registration numbers:	TLP 2439
(vii) house numbers:	1279 Forty-fifth Street

The house number in an address should not be followed by a comma before the street name; and the number of the postal district, if this is in small caps, should be set in non-lining, hanging figures: 221

15 Sutherland Grove, London N.W.7

[not: 15, Sutherland Grove, London, N.W.7]

It is important to see that figures included in an italicized phrase should also be set in italic (not in roman): 222

The Revolution of 1789	not: *The Revolution of* 1789
King Henry VI, Part III	not: *King Henry* VI, *Part* III
1 Henry IV	not: I *Henry* IV

Lower-case roman numerals, rather than either upper-case roman or arabic numerals, may conveniently be used for volume numbers, especially in notes: 223

vol. xxviii *rather than:* Vol. XXVIII *or:* Vol. 28

and also for the month (set between full points) in dates:

3.ix.1913

It will often look better to set small capital roman numerals after the name of a sovereign: 224

Louis XVIII *rather than:* Louis XVIII

When successive paragraphs are introduced by numerals, care should be taken to range the opening words of the text 225 of each successive paragraph, rather than ranging the numerals preceding them:

(i) The party which had gained power . . .	not:	(i) The party which . . .
(ii) Opposed to them were the . . .		(ii) Opposed to them . . .
(iii) Holding the balance between them was . . .		(iii) Holding the . . .

17 DATES

226 In setting dates, avoid commas and contractions as far as possible:

Sunday, 21 May 1865 **not:** Sunday, May 21st, 1865
Tuesday, 14 June **not:** Tuesday, 14th June
before 12 October **not:** before the 12th October
Throughout July 1940 the invasion was expected hourly.
By Christmas 1958 they were not only engaged but married.

227 But where the day of the month only is given, or a date begins a sentence, set as follows:

The 30th had been bitterly cold and wintry. May 1, on the contrary, turned out a glorious spring day. May 1, 1920 had, he remembered, shown just as remarkable a change of weather.

228 Print in full:

from 1934 to 1938 **not:** from 1934–38
between 1919 and 1939 **not:** between 1919–39

229 A.D. precedes the year; B.C. follows the year:

A.D. 1903 753 B.C.
Julius Caesar invaded Britain 55 B.C.

but: William the Conqueror invaded England A.D. 1066

230 Contract years A.D. thus:

A.D. 338–40

but years B.C. must not be contracted, because of the risk of ambiguity:

340–338 B.C. **not:** 340–38 B.C.

Do not contract extent of days of the month: 231

on the night of 23–24 May | not: 23–4 May
on the night of 28–29 August 1948

18 ITALICS

Titles of books, newspapers, periodical publications, poems of book-length (divided into cantos, parts, etc.), plays, operas, oratorios, films are all to be set in italic; also names of ships, aeroplanes and airships: 232

Bleak House
The Strange Case of Dr Jekyll and Mr Hyde
The Observer
the *Guardian*
the *New Statesman*
Blackwood's Magazine
The Canterbury Tales
Dante's *Inferno*
Spenser's *Faerie Queene*
Henry V
The Second Mrs Tanqueray
Strindberg's *The Father*
Gounod's *Faust*
H.M.S. Pinafore
Peter Grimes
Handel's *Messiah*
Bach's *St Matthew Passion*
Chaplin's *The Dictator*
Ben Hur
The Birth of a Nation
H.M.S. *Renown*
s.s. *Queen Mary*
Lindbergh's *Spirit of St Louis*

Hermann Köhl made the first successful east-to-west trans-atlantic flight in the *Bremen*.

the *Graf Zeppelin*

the *R 101*

233 Titles of chapters of books, newspaper articles, short stories, poems of average length, songs, symphonies and shorter musical compositions, ballets, paintings and sculptures should appear in roman within quotes:

'Introductory'

'The Future of Automation'

'The Gioconda Smile'

Milton's 'Ode on the Morning of Christ's Nativity'

Keats's 'Ode on a Grecian Urn'

Eliot's 'The Waste Land'

'The Lost Chord'

'The Lass with a Delicate Air'

the 'Eroica' symphony

the 'Moonlight' sonata

'Swan Lake'

the 'Mona Lisa'

the 'Laocoön'

234 Inns, hotels, great houses, theatres, shipping lines, long-distance trains, and classes of aircraft should be named in roman without quotes:

the Goat and Compasses

the Mason's Arms

the Running Footman

the Spread Eagle

the Ritz

Claridge's

Blenheim Palace

Hardwick Hall

Longleat
Compton Wynyates
the Lyceum
the Prince of Wales Theatre
Her Majesty's
the Curzon cinema
the Cunard line
a P. and O. liner
the Flying Scotsman
the Red Dragon
the Cornish Riviera (Express)
a Spitfire
a Messerschmitt
a Mustang
a Viscount

Some periodicals reckon the definite article as part of their title; it must therefore be likewise italicized: 235

The Birmingham Post
The Chester Chronicle
The Crewe Chronicle
The Cornhill Magazine
The Daily Telegraph (and Morning Post)
The Economist
The Field
The Financial Times
The Irish Times
The Lady
The Lancet
The Listener
The Musical Times
The Nantwich Chronicle
The Observer

The People

The Queen

The Scotsman

The Studio

The Sunday Times

The Tablet

The Tatler & Bystander

The Times (and its Supplements)

The Yorkshire Post

236 Other periodicals do not include the definite article in their title:

the *Birmingham Evening Mail and Despatch*, the *British Weekly*, the *Daily Mail*, the *Economic Review*, the *Guardian**, the *Irish Independent*, the *Jewish Chronicle*, the *New York Herald Tribune*, the *Spectator*, the *Statist*, the *Sun*, the *Sunday Citizen* (*and Reynolds News*), the *Times of India*, etc.

237 It is important to ascertain the style preferred by each individual periodical, and editors always appreciate the courtesy of an inquiry.

238 Note, however, the following usage, even with periodicals requiring *The* in their title:

I read it in one of the *Times* leading articles. **not:** *The Times*'s

According to the *Observer* inquiry, this was shown to be quite untrue.

239 If any of the above titles is abbreviated, it should be set likewise in italic or roman, quoted or unquoted, as already laid down:

What a fascinating story *Jekyll and Hyde* is!

I read a most interesting article in *Blackwood's*.

* Do not be misled by an erroneous rule of thumb which asserts that the style of the front page of the periodical is a safe guide to whether the definite article forms part of the title or not. The *Guardian*'s practice disproves this rule.

The performance of *Pinafore* was rapturously received.

The choir sang Bach's *Matthew Passion* in two parts: before and after lunch.

The loss of the *Renown* was disastrous.

I had been reading Milton's 'Nativity Ode'.

. . . the well-known lines of Keats's 'Grecian Urn' . . .

The guide who showed us round Blenheim was most interesting.

The revue had a long run at the Prince of Wales.

The film we saw at the Curzon was most enjoyable.

Have you seen the current issue of *The Cornhill* yet?

We used to take *The Tatler* every week without fail.

Foreign words occurring in the course of English sentences should normally be set in italic: **240**

There is a certain *je ne sais quoi* about him.

We found ourselves at once *en rapport*.

She had such *joie de vivre*.

We stayed in a comfortable *Gasthaus*.

I am very fond of *Pumpernickel*.

Lifting his glass, he said *Prosit!* and drank my health.

the *Sturm und Drang* school of writers

I found him living in a lovely Venetian *palazzo*.

Whether it's true or not, it is certainly *ben trovato*!

It was the *conquistadores* who blazed the trail.

I was sitting there, enjoying a delicious *paella*.

The rebels' first act was to issue a *pronunciamiento*.

She was a simple, unlettered *gitana*.

Viva la Reina! was the cry heard on all sides.

There were many other Castilian *pueblos* we visited.

Before saying the *Ite, missa est*, the priest gave the blessing.

His *floruit* as a writer was round about the '70s.

This hapless, inoffensive tourist was dragged before the *cadi*.

241 Many foreign words, however, have been adopted as normal English usage and should therefore be set in roman:

Anschluss	mêlée
belles-lettres	migraine
blasé	mistral
bourgeois	motif
brassière	persiflage
buffet	pietà
chic	pince-nez
cul-de-sac	précis
dachshund	protégé(e)
débâcle	rendezvous
debris	role
denouement	sang-froid
doyen	siesta
fichu	soi-disant
hacienda	soirée
hauteur	soupçon
inamorato (-a)	suède
levee	umlaut
matinée	Zeitgeist

Note that the accent, hyphen, or initial capital letter is required by usage in some of these words, but not in others.

242 Foreign sentences occurring in dialogue are, of course, to be set in normal roman type:

'Mille mercis', she exclaimed; 'vous êtes très gentil!'

243 Foreign titles of address in common use are to be set in roman:

Monsieur	Signor	Señor	Herr
Madame	Signora	Señora	Frau

Mademoiselle	Signorina	Señorita	Fräulein
Comte	Contessa		Freiherr
	Marchese		Graf
	Duce		Gräfin
	Duchessa		

Latin abbreviations should be set in roman: 244

e.g. i.e. cp. cf. v. (*vide*) q.v. viz.
sq. sqq. id. ibid. op. cit. loc. cit.

but italicize: *c.* (*circa*) *v.* (*versus*) *et al.*

The possessive *s* following an italicized word should be set in roman with its apostrophe: 245

all the *New Statesman*'s readers

the whole of the *Victory*'s crew

The Observer's correspondence columns

Italic may be used for words or letters mentioned by name: 246

'Surely the use of *is* is wrong here? It ought to be *are*.' 'Well, I'm afraid I meant *is*.'

In English the letter *q* is invariably followed by *u*.

Italic may also be used for the purpose of emphasis, but with restraint. Few things are more tiring or exasperating to the reader than repeated emphasis, which is a mark of poverty of style. 247

If words not originally emphasized in quoted matter are italicized by author or editor, this fact must be scrupulously noted by a phrase inserted in brackets:

[italics mine—H.R.]

or: [italics ours—eds]

or: [italics not in original—Author]

248 Words which, according to the foregoing rules, are to be italicized in roman text are conversely to be set in roman if they occur in an italic text:

Extract from a diary:

Friday, 19th. *Have just read in the* Spectator *of enthusiastic reception of* Oklahoma *last night. Obviously a* succès fou. *It will be interesting to read what* The People *has to say about it on Sunday.*

249 Care must be taken to see that punctuation marks are italicized only if they belong strictly to an italicized word or phrase preceding them; if the punctuation mark belongs to the whole sentence, it must be set in roman:

'*Mon Dieu!*', exclaimed the marquise, 'where have I left my – how do you call it? – my *parapluie*?'

'Drinks for everyone, did you say? Including the *children*?'

. . . the lovely line that ends *Paradise Lost*: 'Through Eden took their solitary way.'

19 FOREIGN NAMES

250 Prefixes such as *de*, *von*, *van*, forming part of proper names, are normally to be set in lower case:

Alfred de Musset General de Gaulle Mme de Staël
Friedrich von Hügel Baroness von Hutten zum Stolzenberg
Ludwig Joachim von Arnim Vincent van Gogh
Hendrik van Loon Jan van den Bosch

They are of course to be capitalized if they begin a sentence:

Van Gogh was born four years before de Musset died.

251 When, however, such a name has come to be reckoned as English, the personal style of the bearer of the name must be followed:

	but:
Baron De La Warr	Walter de la Mare
Thomas De Quincey	Sir Humphrey de Trafford
William De Morgan	Sir Beauvoir de Lisle
Viscount D'Abernon	Eamon de Valera

Note also:

Norman Del Mar	John Van Druten
Martin Van Buren	Sir Anthony Van Dyck
Carl Van Doren	David Van Nostrand

In German proper names the umlaut should not normally be omitted or replaced by another form: 252

Göring **[not:** Goering**]** Düsseldorf **[not:** Duesseldorf**]**

Where these forms are likely to occur, care should be taken in the choice of fount.

On the other hand, the umlaut must not be introduced where it does not belong: 253

Goebbels **[not:** Göbbels**]** Goethe **[not:** Göthe**]**
Ernst H. Haeckel **[not:** Häckel**]**

'*t* (abbreviated from *het*), forming part of a Dutch name, should not be set close up to the preceding or following word: 254

Jacobus Hendricus van 't Hoff
[not: van't Hoff **nor:** van 'tHoff **]**
Willem Visser 't Hooft
[not: Visser't Hooft **nor:** Visser 'tHooft**]**

In Dutch words, *ij* is treated as a single compound letter. When it is the initial letter of a proper noun, both *i* and *j* must be capitalized: 255

IJsbrechtum	IJsselsteijn
IJsselmuiden	IJzendijke

256 The following list of geographical names shows their distinctive forms in various languages. (Note that some English forms are given which, though strictly incorrect, are supported by long usage.) Local forms are printed in bold type.

English	*French*	*German*	*Other forms*
Adrianople	Adrinople	Adrianopel	**Edirne** (Turkish)
Agincourt	**Azincourt**		
Alderney	Aurigny		
Alsace	**L'Alsace**	Elsass	
Andalusia	Andalousie	Andalusien	**Andalucía** (Spanish)
Anspach		**Ansbach**	
Antananarivo	Tananarive		**Tananarivo** (Malagasy)
Antwerp	**Anvers**	Antwerpen	**Antwerpen** (Flemish)
Apennines	Les Apennins	Apenninen	**Appennino** (Italian)
Apulia	La Pouille Les Pouilles	Apulien	**Puglia** (Italian)
Aragon		Aragonien	**Aragón** (Spanish)
Archangel			**Arkhangelsk** (Russian)
Athens	Athènes	Athen	**Athinai** (Greek)
Azores, The	**Les Açores**	Azoren	**Açores** (Portuguese)
Basle	**Bâle**	**Basel**	
Bavaria	La Bavière	**Bayern**	
Beirut	Beyrouth		
Belgrade		Belgrad	**Beograd** (Serbian)
Berne	**Berne**	**Bern**	
Biscay	**La Biscaye**	Biskaya	
Biscay, Bay of	**Le Golfe de Gascogne**		
Blenheim		**Blindheim**	
Bohemia	La Bohème	Böhmen	**Čechy** (Czech)
Brill, The			**Briel**, **Brielle**, **Bril** (Dutch)
Brittany	**La Bretagne**		
Bruges	**Bruges**	Brügge	**Brugge** (Flemish)
Brunswick		**Braunschweig**	
Brussels	**Bruxelles**	Brüssel	**Brussel** (Flemish)
Bucharest	Bucarest		**Bucureşti** (Romanian)
Burgundy	**La Bourgogne**	Burgund	
Cadiz	Cadix		**Cádiz** (Spanish) Cadice (Italian)
Cairo	Le Caire	Kairo	**al-Qâhirah** (Arabic)
Cambray	**Cambrai**		Kambryk (Flemish)
Camperdown			**Kamp**, **Kamperduin**, **Camperduin** (Dutch)
Canterbury	Cantorbéry		

English	*French*	*German*	*Other forms*
Carinthia	La Carinthie	**Kärnten**	Carinzia (Italian)
Carpathians	Les Carpathes	Karpaten	**Karpaty** (Czech, Polish) Carpaţii (Romanian)
Cashmere	Le Cachemire		**Kashmir** (Hindi)
Castile	La Castille	Kastilien	**Castilla** (Spanish)
Catalonia	La Catalogne	Katalonien	**Catalunya** (Catalan) **Cataluña** (Spanish)
Cawnpore			**Kanpur** (Hindi)
Christiansand			**Kristiansand** (Norwegian)
Christiansund			**Kristiansund** (Norwegian)
Cleves	Clèves	**Cleve, Kleve**	
Coblenz	Coblence	**Koblenz**	
Cologne	Cologne	**Köln**	
Connaught		Connacht	**Connacht** (Irish)
Copenhagen	Copenhague	Kopenhagen	**København** (Danish)
Cordova	Cordoue	Kordova	**Córdoba** (Spanish)
Corsica	**La Corse**	Korsika	
Corunna	La Corogne		**La Coruña** (Spanish)
Cracow	Cracovie	Krakau	**Kraków** (Polish)
Cressy	**Crécy**		
Crete	La Crète	**Kreta**	**Kriti** (Greek)
Crimea, The	La Crimée		**Krim** (Russian)
Croatia	La Croatie	Kroatien	**Hrvatska** (Serbo-Croat)
Czechoslovakia	La Tchécoslovaquie	Tschechoslowakei	**Československo** (Czech)
Dalmatia	La Dalmatie	Dalmatien	**Dalmacija** (Serbo-Croat)
Danube, R.	Le Danube	**Donau**	**Duna** (Hungarian) **Dunarea** (Romanian)
Danzig	**Dantzig**	**Danzig**	**Gdańsk** (Polish)
Delphi	Delphes	Delphi	**Delphoi** (Greek)
Denmark	Le Danemark	Dänemark	**Danmark** (Danish)
Dnieper, R.		Dnjepr	**Dnepr** (Russian)
Dniester, R.		Dnjestr	**Dnestr** (Russian)
Dover	Douvres		
Doway	**Douai**		
Dunkirk	**Dunkerque**	Dünkirchen	
Edinburgh	Édimbourg	Edinburg	Edimburgo (Italian)
Elsinore	Elseneur	Helsingör	**Helsingør** (Danish)
Estonia	L'Esthonie	Estland	**Eesti** (Estonian)
Euphrates, R.	L'Euphrate	Euphrat	**Firat, Frat** (Turkish) Al Furât (Arabic)
Faeroes, The	Les îles Féroé	Faröer	**Föroyar** (Færoese) Færoerne (Danish)
Fez	Fès	Fez	**Fas** (Arabic)
Finland	La Finlande	Finnland	**Suomi** (Finnish)
Flanders	**La Flandre**	Flandern	**Vlaanderen** (Flemish)
Florence	Florence	Florenz	**Firenze** (Italian)

English	*French*	*German*	*Other forms*
Flushing	Flessingue	Vlissingen	**Vlissingen** (Dutch)
Fontarabia			**Fuenterrabia** (**Spanish**)
Franconia		**Franken**	
Frankfort	Francfort	**Frankfurt**	
Galicia (Poland)	La Galicie	Galizien	**Halicz** (Polish)
Galicia (Spain)	La Galice	Galicien	**Galicia** (Spanish)
Gallipoli			**Gelibolu** (Turkish)
Ganges, R.	Le Gange	Ganges	**Ganga** (Hindi)
Gascony	**La Gascogne**		
Genappe	**Genappe**		**Genepiën** (Flemish)
Geneva	**Genève**	**Genf**	**Genevra** (Romansh) Ginevra (Italian)
Genoa	Gênes	Genua	**Genova** (Italian)
Ghent	**Gand**	Gent	**Gent** (Flemish)
Greenland	Le Groenland	Grönland	**Grönland** (Danish) Groenlandia (Italian)
Guernsey	Guernesey		
Guinea	**La Guinée**		**Guinea** (Spanish) **Guiné** (Portuguese)
Hague, The	La Haye	Der Haag	**'s Gravenhage** **den Haag** } (Dutch
Hainault	**Hainaut**	Hennegau	**Henegouwen** (Flemish)
Haiti	**Haïti**		
Hamburg	Hambourg	**Hamburg**	
Hamelin		**Hameln**	
Hanover	Hanovre	**Hannover**	
Hapsburg		**Habsburg**	
Havana	La Havane	Havanna	**La Habana** (Spanish)
Havre	**Le Havre**		
Heligoland		**Helgoland**	
Hesse		**Hessen**	Assia (Italian)
Hungary	La Hongrie	Ungarn	**Magyarország** (Hungarian)
Iceland	L'Islande	Island	**Ísland** (Icelandic) Island (Danish)
Jersey	Jersey		
Jutland			**Jylland** (Danish)
Lapland	La Laponie	Lappland	**Lapland** (Norwegian) **Lappi** (Finnish) **Lappland** (Swedish)
Latvia	La Lettonie		**Latvija** (Lettish)
Leghorn	Livourne	Livorno	**Livorno** (Italian)
Leyden	Leyde	Leiden	**Leiden** (Dutch)
Liège	**Liège**	Lüttich	**Luik** (Flemish)

English	*French*	*German*	*Other forms*
Limburg	**Limbourg**		**Limburg** (Flemish and Dutch)
Lions, Gulf of	**Golfe du Lion**		
Lisbon	Lisbonne	Lissabon	**Lisboa** (Portuguese) Lisbona (Italian)
Lithuania	La Lituanie	Litauen	**Lietuva** (Lithuanian)
Lombardy	La Lombardie	Lombardei	**Lombardia** (Italian)
London	Londres		Londra (Italian)
Lorraine	**La Lorraine**	Lothringen	
Louvain	**Louvain**	Löwen	**Leuven** (Flemish)
Lucerne	**Lucerne**	**Luzern**	**Lucerna** (Italian)
Luxemburg	**Luxembourg**	Luxemburg	
Lyons	**Lyon**	Lyon	
Macedonia	Macédoine	Mazedonien	**Makedonia** (Greek)
Madeira	Madère		**Madeira** (Portuguese)
Main, R.	Mein	**Main**	
Mainz	Mayence	**Mainz**	
Majorca	Majorque		**Mallorca** (Spanish)
Malaga			**Málaga** (Spanish)
Mantua	Mantoue		**Mantova** (Italian)
Marseilles	**Marseille**		
Mecca	La Mecque	Mekka	**Makka** (Arabic)
Mechlin	**Malines**	Mecheln	**Mechelen** (Flemish)
Medina	Médine		**al-Madina** (Arabic)
Meknes	**Meknès**		Mequinez (Spanish)
Menin	**Menin**		**Meenen** (Flemish)
Meuse, R.	**Meuse**	Maas	**Maas** (Dutch)
Mexico	Le Mexique	Mexiko	**México** (Mexican Spanish) Méjico (Spanish) Messico (Italian)
Milan	Milan	Mailand	**Milano** (Italian)
Minorca	Minorque		**Menorca** (Spanish)
Moldavia	La Moldavie	Moldau	**Moldova** (Romanian)
Moluccas, The	Les Moluques	Molukken	**Molukken** (Dutch)
Mons	**Mons**		**Bergen** (Flemish)
Moravia	Moravie	Mähren	**Morava** (Czech)
Moscow	Moscou	Moskau	**Moskva** (Russian)
Moselle, R.	**Moselle**	**Mosel**	
Mozambique			**Moçambique** (Portuguese)
Mulhausen	**Mulhouse**	Mülhausen	
Munich		**München**	Monaco (Italian)
Naples		Neapel	**Napoli** (Italian)
Normandy	**La Normandie**		Normandia (Italian)
Norway	La Norvège	Norwegen	**Norge** (Norwegian) Norvegia (Italian)
Nuremberg		**Nürnberg**	
Nymegen	Nimègue	Nimwegen	**Nijmegen** (Dutch)

English	*French*	*German*	*Other forms*
Oporto	Porto		**Pôrto** (Portuguese)
Orleans	**Orléans**		Orleans (Italian)
Osnaburg(h)		**Osnabrück**	
Ostend	**Ostende**	Ostende	**Oostende** (Flemish)
Oudenarde	**Audenarde**		**Oudenaarde** (Flemish)
Padua	Padoue		**Padova** (Italian)
Picardy	**La Picardie**		
Piedmont	Le Piémont	Piemont	**Piemonte** (Italian)
Piraeus, The	Le Pirée	Piräus	**Peiraievs** (Greek)
			Pireo (Italian)
Plate, R.			**Río de la Plata** (Spanish)
Poland	La Pologne	Polen	**Polska** (Polish)
			Polonia (Italian)
Pomerania	La Poméranie	**Pommern**	
Pompeii	Pompéi	Pompeji	**Pompei** (Italian)
Posen			**Poznań** (Polish)
Prague	Prague	Prag	**Praha** (Czech)
Prussia	La Prusse	**Preussen**	
Pyrenees	**Les Pyrénées**	Pyrenäen	**Pirineos** (Spanish)
			Pirenei (Italian)
Ratisbon	Ratisbonne	**Regensburg**	
Rheims	**Reims**		
Rhine, R.	Rhin	**Rhein**	**Rijn** (Dutch)
			Reno (Italian)
Rhodes		Rhodus	**Rodos** (Greek)
			Rodi (Italian)
Rhone, R.	**Rhône**	Rhone	Rodano (Italian)
Romania	La Roumanie	Rumänien	**România** (Romanian)
			Romania (Italian)
Rome	Rome	Rom	**Roma** (Italian)
Roncesvalles	Roncevaux		**Roncesvalles** (Spanish)
Russia	La Russie	Russland	**Rossiya** (Russian)
Ryswick			**Rijswijk** (Dutch)
Saar, R.	**Sarre**	**Saar**	
Saint Gall	**Saint-Gall**	**Sankt Gallen**	
Saragossa	Saragosse		**Zaragoza** (Spanish)
Sardinia	La Sardaigne	Sardinien	**Sardegna** (Italian)
Sark	Sercq		
Savoy	**Savoie**	Savoyen	**Savoia** (Italian)
Saxony	La Saxe	**Sachsen**	Sassonia (Italian)
Scheldt, R.	**Escaut**	Schelde	**Schelde** (Flemish)
Scilly, Isles of	Les Sorlingues	Scilly-inseln	Isole Sorlinghe (Italian)
Senegal	**Le Sénégal**	Senegal	
Seville	Séville	Sevilla	**Sevilla** (Spanish)
Shlisselburg		Schlüsselburg	**Shlisselburg** (Russian)
Sienna	Sienne		**Siena** (Italian)

English	*French*	*German*	*Other forms*
Silesia	La Silésie	**Schlesien**	**Slezsko** (Czech)
			Śląsk (Polish)
			Slesia (Italian)
Sinai	Sinaï		**Sina** (Arabic)
Sleswick	Slesvig	**Schleswig**	**Sleswig** (Danish)
Sluis	L'Écluse		**Sluijs** (Dutch)
Smalcald		**Schmalkalden**	
Smyrna	Smyrne		**Izmir** (Turkish)
Sofia			**Sofiya** (Bulgarian)
Spires	Spire	**Speyer**	
Spitsbergen	Spitzberg		**Svalbard** (Norwegian)
Steinkirk	**Steenkerque**		**Steenkerke** (Flemish)
Strasburg	**Strasbourg**	Strassburg	
Styria	La Styrie	**Steiermark**	
Sudan, The	Le Soudan	Sudan	**Bilâd-es-Sudan** (Arabic)
Swabia	La Souabe	**Schwaben**	
Sweden	La Suède	Schweden	**Sverige** (Swedish)
			Svezia (Italian)
Switzerland	**La Suisse**	**Schweiz**	**Svizzera** (Italian)
			Svizzra (Romansh)
Syracuse		Syrakus	**Siracusa** (Italian)
Tagus, R.	**Le Tage**		**Tajo** (Spanish)
			Tejo (Portuguese)
			Tago (Italian)
Teneriffe		Teneriffa	**Tenerife** (Spanish)
Thames, R.	La Tamise	Themse	Tamigi (Italian)
Thuringia	Thuringe	**Thüringen**	
Tiber, R.	Le Tibre	Tiber	**Tevere** (Italian)
Timbuctoo	**Tombouctou**	Timbuktu	Timbuktu (Italian)
Tirol	Tyrol	**Tirol**	**Tirolo** (Italian)
Tokay			**Tokaj** (Hungarian)
Tournay	**Tournai**		**Doornik** (Flemish)
Transylvania	La Transylvanie	Siebenbürgen	**Transilvania** (Romanian)
			Erdély (Hungarian)
Trent	Trente	Trient	**Trento** (Italian)
Treves	Trèves	**Trier**	
Turin		Turin	**Torino** (Italian)
Turkey	La Turquie	Türkei	**Türkiye** (Turkish)
			Turchia (Italian)
Tuscany	La Toscane	Toskana	**Toscana** (Italian)
Tyre	Tyr, Sour	Tyrus	**Es Sur** (Arabic)
Upsala	Upsal	Upsala	**Uppsala** (Swedish)
Ushant	**L'île d'Ouessant**		**Enez Eusa** (Breton)
Valais	**Valais**	**Wallis**	
Valparaiso			**Valparaíso** (Spanish)
Venice	Venise	Venedig	**Venezia** (Italian)
Vesuvius	Le Vésuve	Vesuv	**Vesuvio** (Italian)

English	*French*	*German*	*Other forms*
Vienna	Vienne	**Wien**	
Vistula, R.	Vistule	Weichsel	**Wisła** (Polish)
			Visla (Russian)
Walachia	La Valachie	Walachei	**Valahia** (Romanian)
Warsaw	Varsovie	Warschau	**Warszawa** (Polish)
Westphalia	La Westphalie	**Westfalen**	
Zagreb		Agram	**Zagreb** (Croat)
			Zágráb (Hungarian)
Zealand		Seeland	**Sjælland** (Danish)
Zeeland	Zélande	Seeland	**Zeeland** (Dutch)
Zurich	**Zurich**	**Zürich**	Zurigo (Italian)
Zuyder Zee	Le Zuyderzée	Zuidersee	**Zuider Zee** (Dutch)

20 ACCENT, DIACRITIC, DIAERESIS, UMLAUT

257 Accents and diacritical marks must be set in accordance with the usage of the language quoted. This applies not only to French and German but no less strictly to Spanish, Portuguese, Italian, Albanian, Serbo-Croat, Hungarian, Romanian, Czech, Polish, and the Baltic and Scandinavian languages.

258 The only accent used in English is the grave accent, which is used not to modify the vowel sound but to indicate that a syllable is to be pronounced which might otherwise be silent:

blessèd (not to be pronounced: blest)

learnèd agèd well-belovèd

the goddess Athenè

the early Christian love feast or *agapè*

'Hence, loathèd Melancholy, . . . '

Note that the acute accent is **not** to be used for this purpose:

blesséd loathéd are **wrong**

259 The diaeresis and the umlaut, though identical in form, are quite distinct in function.

The diaeresis placed over one of two adjacent vowels indicates that it is not to be coalesced with the other but sounded independently of it. 260

It is seldom used in the British Isles except in such words as are still considered to be foreign:

aërial	Boötes
coöperate	Lagües
coördinate	Laocoön
oölite	naïve
oölogy	Noël
preëminent	Pasiphaë
preëmption	Sigüenza
zoölogical	Thaïs

North Americans might use the diaeresis in all the above words; in this country it would be used, if at all, only in the words in the right-hand column. In some of the words in the left-hand column the function of the diaeresis is performed by a hyphen:

co-operate pre-eminent pre-emption

The following words illustrate the English aversion to the use of the diaeresis: 261

coalition	Croatian
coeval	poet
coition	reagent
diet	retroactive

The umlaut is literally a 'sound-change' and is essential to the intelligibility of the word, written or spoken. 262

In German, for example:

schon means 'already'

schön means 'beautiful'

Handel means 'trade'

Händel either means 'trades'
or is the name of the composer

21 ABBREVIATIONS AND CONTRACTIONS

263 Both abbreviations and contractions are ways of shortening a word.

The abbreviation stops short and omits the end of the word.

The contraction telescopes the word by retaining its beginning and end and omitting the middle.

264 An abbreviation should normally end with a full point:

M. MM. Co. Rev. Esq. sen. jun. etc. st. (stanza) p. Hon. cf. cp. viz. fig. id. ibid. f. ff. gal. in. MS. MSS. *s.* *d.* m. (million) n. (note)

265 A contraction always includes the final letter of the word, and should normally have no full point after it:

Mr Mrs Dr Revd Esqre Ltd Coy St (Street, Saint) Ste Mt Mts Mme Mlle Messrs ft 1st 4to 8vo cwt hr pt qt yd Mgr Honble Bt*

266 The two preceding paragraphs state the general rule; but for the sake of clarity there may be exceptions to it in either direction.

267 The following, though contractions, will have the full point:

No. Nos.

268 The following abbreviations, on the other hand, will have no full point:

lb per cent oz

Even in his prep school days, he couldn't behave like a gent if he tried.

Similarly with other abbreviated forms which now are accepted as normal words:

exam gym lab vet rep sub turps

* This contraction, originally in the form 'B^{t}', is more widely in use than 'Bart', and is preferred by the Committee of the Standing Council of the Baronetage.

Abbreviated personal names, whether forenames or surnames, do not take the full point:

Alf Di Herb Mac Reg Stan Theo Vic

The following do not end with *s* in the plural: **269**

cwt oz gm cm. mm. gr. in. min. sec.

The following take final *s* in the plural, without full point: **270**

lbs gals pts qts yds hrs

Certain abbreviations take a full point only at the end: **271**

PS. MS. MSS. fn.

Abbreviations such as the following: **272**

i.e. cf. cp. p. pp. op. cit. loc. cit. id. ibid. e.g. viz. *c.* *v.*

may be set in lower case, even at the beginning of a sentence.

In general writing, avoid abbreviations in the form of symbols: **273**

5 per cent **not:** 5 %

2*s.* **not:** 2/– 3*s.* 6½*d.* **not:** 3/6½

Such symbols may, however, be necessary in setting statistics, tabular matter, and so forth.

The symbol '£' is not followed by a full point, but immediately precedes the figure. If, however, '*l.*' is used, it is to be set in italic after the figure and followed by a full point: **274**

£5 4*s.* 2½*d.* 5*l.* 4*s.* 2½*d.*

Always print 'etc.' (**not** '&c.' unless specifically instructed to do so). **275**

Do not print 'etc., etc'. It is a meaningless duplication.

Restrict the use of the ampersand to the names of those companies, institutions, etc. which officially require it. The heading of their notepaper will usually give the necessary **276** indication. Do not be guided by the Telephone Directory, which naturally makes use of condensed forms.

The following are examples:

Allen & Hanburys	George Allen and Unwin
G. Bell & Sons Ltd	Hodder and Stoughton
Secker & Warburg	Lilley and Skinner
Longmans, Green & Co. Limited	Marks and Spencer
Gerald Duckworth & Co. Ltd	Thames and Hudson

If in doubt, do not use the ampersand.

An ampersand should not begin or end a line.

277 Shortened forms consisting only of initial letters, if pronounced as single words, should appear in caps, without medial or concluding full points:

UNO NATO UNRRA OGPU SEATO
SHAPE SHAEF RAF WOSB NALGO

278 Where other than initial letters appear in the compound word, set in upper and lower case:

Gestapo Aslib Natsopa Aslef Comintern Benelux

279 Full points are to be used in such abbreviations as

U.N. U.S.A. U.S.S.R. U.A.R. N.U.R.

but not in the following:

BBC TV ATV ITV Tb ABC (Railway Guide)

nor in versions of the Bible:

AV RV RSV NEB JB

22 A OR AN?

280 When the indefinite article precedes an abbreviation consisting of initial letters, be guided by the spoken sound:

	but:
a U.N. resolution	an UNNRA undertaking
a BBC programme	an R.C. priest

a RAF-type moustache	an R.A.F. base
a UNICEF greeting card	

Similarly, the spoken sound may dictate the use of *a* (rather than *an*) even before a word beginning with a vowel: 281

a one-time beauty   a European   a Unionist politician

The use of *an* before certain words beginning with *h* (even when aspirated) has now become rare. Such expressions as *an hotel*, *an historic event*, *an hundredweight*, are increasingly regarded as old-fashioned. 282

But the usage persists in certain instances:

	but:
a habit	an habitual distaste
a halberdier	an hallucination
a harbinger	an harangue
a harmony of sweet sounds	an harmonica
a harrow	an Harrovian
a hurry	an hurrah
a hussy	an hussar
a hypnotist	an hypothesis
a hypocrite	an hysterical outburst

It will appear that stress has a good deal to do with it.

23 O OR OH?

O is to be used in the vocative case, and in sentences in which it is not itself stressed: 283

O come, all ye faithful

O piteous spectacle! O noble Caesar!

O Lord, save the Queen.

284 *Oh* should be used only when emphatic and exclamatory. It is usually, but not always, followed immediately by a mark of punctuation:

Oh, shut up!

Oh! I'm hurt!

When, oh when, will he come?

24 ONE WORD OR TWO?

285 Certain pairs of words are so commonly associated that they are apt to be mistakenly set as a single word – which, incidentally, may bear a meaning very different from the one intended. The examples below will illustrate this error:

286 *Altogether, all together*

There were the children all together, playing happily. There must have been forty or fifty of them altogether.

287 *Already, all ready*

'I'll come down when I hear they're all ready prepared.'
'But I'm telling you – they *are* already prepared, and waiting.'

288 *Awhile, a while*

'Well, I'm afraid they'll have to wait for a while.'

[**not:** for awhile]

'Wait awhile! I won't be a moment.'

289 *Anyone, any one*

I have never known anyone of his age so devoted to study; he looked through the shelves and said he'd love to have any one of the historical works for his prize.

but: . . . any of the historical works for his prizes.

290 *Everyone, every one*

Everyone who had given any help in the rescue was there. The mayor presented every one of them with a gold watch and chain.

'Oh, I can look after every one of the *children* all right. But I really can't cope with *everyone* – fathers, mothers, uncles, aunts, and nurses as well!'

Someone, some one **291**

'Will each of you select some one of these specimens, take it away, and get on with your individual experiment. If you want any help or advice, I'll see that there's someone to give it you.'

Sometime, some time **292**

'He was sometime professor at Aberdeen University.'
'Ah, I think I remember seeing him there some time back. Now that he's down south, I'll look him up some time.'

The date of Zoroaster seems to have been some time in the first half of the sixth century B.C.

Some time previously I had warned him.

However, how ever **293**

'But how ever did you get away?'
'I didn't; however frantically I struggled, I couldn't get free.'

Anyway, any way **294**

'. . . And anyway, I thought, why make the effort? I know that before I could get any way down the street, the hue and cry would be raised, and then . . . ?'

Whatever, what ever **295**

'What ever are you fussing about?'
[not: 'Whatever are you fussing about?']

'How dreadful! What ever did you reply?'
'What could I reply? Whatever I said was bound to give offence.'

Whoever, who ever **296**

At the sound of the doorbell he started and exclaimed, 'Who ever's that?' I said I had no idea. 'Well, whoever it is', he said, 'mustn't find *me* here.'

297 *Whenever, when ever*

'When ever did you get here, and why ever have you been waiting in this cheerless room all by yourself?'
'My dear man, I knew perfectly well that, whenever I arrived, you'd be too busy to see me immediately. So I just waited.'

298 *Wherever, where ever*

Wherever I turned, I was faced with disaster.

Let our soules flie to th' shades, where ever springs
Sit smiling in the Meads; . . .
—Herrick, 'The Apparition of his Mistresse'

25 SPELLINGS

299 Consult the authorities listed in Section 1, and note that where CHAMBERS gives alternative spellings the first is usually to be preferred: except the ending -ise (see below, 306).

300 Preferred spellings:

	rather than:
abridgement	abridgment
absinth	absinthe
acknowledgement	acknowledgment
ageing	aging
alignment	alinement
baccara	baccarat
balk	baulk
biased	biassed
blonde	blond
caviare	caviar
centring	centering
chancellery	chancellory
chevy	chivy, chivvy
cider	cyder
cipher	cypher
coconut	coco-nut
connexion	connection
cony	coney

	rather than:
develop(ment)	develope(ment)
dexterous	dextrous
dike	dyke
dispatch	despatch
dryly	drily
envelop(ment)	envelope(ment)
but: envelope (noun)	
fiord	fjord
fledgling	fledgeling
flu	'flu
focused	focussed
forebear (ancestor)	forbear
for ever	forever
garrotte	garotte
genuflexion	genuflection
gerry (slang for German)	jerry
gerrymander	jerrymander
guerrilla	guerilla
imbroglio	embroglio
inflexion	inflection
inquire inquiry	enquire enquiry
jail jailer	gaol gaoler
jewellery	jewelry
judgement	judgment
knowledgeable	knowledgable
kotow	kowtow
largess	largesse
loath	loth
lodgement	lodgment
lour	lower
macintosh	mackintosh
marquess	marquis
naught	nought
orang-utan	orang-outang
phone	'phone
plane	'plane
premiss (in logic)	premise

	rather than:
raja	rajah
reflection	reflexion
ripost	riposte
scathless	scatheless
sill	cill
sillabub	syllabub
siphon	syphon
spongeing	sponging
storey	story
totalisator	totalizator
tyke	tike
tyre	tire
veranda	verandah
wagon	waggon
wistaria	wisteria

301 Difficult spellings:

abscess	buses	independent
accidentally		indistinguishable
accommodate	calendar	instil
admissible	calibre	interpretative
aeroplane	calligraphy	
agenda	callisthenics	knick-knack
agreeable	camellia	
all right	carburettor	liquefy
almanac	Caribbean	
already	cemetery	matey
annul	chagrined	moccasin
appalling		
apparel	desiccate	numskull
apparent		
asinine	forbear (verb)	paraffin
aught	forgather	pedlar (U.S. peddler)
	fulfil(ment)	pell-mell
banister		per cent
battalion	haemorrhage	Pharaoh
bookkeeping	horsy	Philippines
boycott		phoney
brand-new	idolater	physiognomy

pick-a-back	recompense	sauerkraut
plaid	ropy	sola topi
plasticine		
plough (U.S. plow)	satellite	tonsillitis

Compared spellings: 302

acceptable susceptible
forcible unenforceable
impassable impassible
implacable irreplaceable
impracticable unpractical

apostasy intimacy
autocracy bureaucracy idiosyncrasy
ecstasy privacy

assistance insistence
resistance resistant irresistible
resister transistor
persistence subsistence
pretence pretension pretentious

stationary stationery
accessary accessory
dignitary signatory
proprietary proprietor(ial)
summary summery
chancellor chancellery
sultry desultory

licence (noun) license (verb)
practice (noun) practise (verb)
prophecy (noun) prophesy (verb)

dickey dicky
matey horsy
honey phoney

cast caste
grill grille
lath lathe
loath loathe loathsome
moral morale
airborne newborn seaborne

embarrass harass harry
offered proffered preferred
corrugated coruscated
irradiating iridescent

callus callous
mucus mucous
phosphorus phosphorous

bias biased
focus focused

budgeting riveting curvetting befitting benefiting

raging ageing dying dyeing swinging swingeing

clarion clarinet marionette

rhododendron rodomontade
mendacity mendicity
panoply monopoly
Jim Crow gimcrack gymnastics
uncharted unchartered
tarantella tarantula
misogamist misogynist
draft draught
straightened straitened
mantel(piece) dismantle
discomfit discomfort
meter metre
datum data
candelabrum candelabra
dependent dependant
entitle intitule
principal principle
glutinous gluttonous
freeze frieze
sonneteer profiteer privateer muleteer gazetteer
desert dessert
cirrhosis cirrus
noggin egg-nog
hangar hanger

stratum strata
tier weir weird
comity committee
pollen pollinate
hussy hussar huzza
blouse blowzy
lackey lacquer
carousal carousel
faun fawn
satyr satire
religious sacrilegious
pidgin pigeon widgeon
dungeon dudgeon burgeon luncheon puncheon
affect effect
ensure insure
divergences emergencies
excellences Excellencies
unravelled unparalleled
Appalachians Apennines
Carmarthen Caernarvon
Johannesburg Johannisberg
Nassau Nyasa Nyanza

brachet ratchet crochet crotchet

motet quartet septet sestet sextet octet omelet

misspelt misstated misled mizzled

paean paeon peon peony

Griselda Grizel grisly gristly grizzled grizzly

azure embrasure brazier

exercise exorcize

forecastle fo'c'sle

two famous sons of Devon: Uncle Tom Cobbleigh
Sir Walter Ralegh

scull skull
filter philtre
fillip Philip
canvas canvass

assuage gauge
interpellate interpolate
lineament liniment
literal littoral
liquor liqueur
trooper trouper
dumbfounded numskull
appraise apprise
nation damnation Dalmatian Alsatian
Caribbean desiccate
autarchy autarky
aneurysm paroxysm

tentative preventive
interpretative repetitive
qualitative quantitative
sensitive normative

syllable sillabub
Sybil Sibylline
typhoon siphon

cede intercede supersede supercilious
precede proceed

forbear (verb) forebear (noun)
forgo forego
forgather forfeit

artefact artificial
beautify liquefy
rarefied stupefied

complement(ary) compliment(ary)
implement sediment

annul annulment
fulfil fulfilment
instil enthral
install instalment
thrall thraldom
fullness fulsome
spell dispel
galop gallop
channelled paralleled
fuselage fusillade

canon cannon canonize cannonade
dragonnade fanfaronade gasconade

stallion battalion
pillion postilion
million vermilion

millionaire questionnaire
millenary millennial
centenary centennial
millinery Millenarianism

council(lor) counsel(lor)

Oxford College: Magdalen
Cambridge College: Magdalene

Beverley, Yorks.
Beverly Hills, Cal.

Hertford, Eng.
Hartford, Conn.

Newhaven, Sussex
New Haven, Conn.

candour clangor languor
colour coloration colourist decolour decolorize
humour humorous liquor odour deodorant malodorous
rigour rigorous ***rigor mortis*** **pallor squalor tremor**
vapour vaporous

sulphur sulphurous

Spelling of certain titles **303**

Note the divergence between the spelling of certain titles and that of the places from which they may be thought, sometimes erroneously, to be derived:

Aylesbury:	Ailesbury is the title of the marquessate hereditary in the Brudenell-Bruce family.
Caernarvon:	Carnarvon is the title of the earldom hereditary in the Herbert family.
Cromarty:	Cromartie is the title of the barony hereditary in the Mackenzie family.

Donegal:	Donegall is the title of the marquessate hereditary in the Chichester family.
Guildford:	Guilford is the title of the earldom hereditary in the North family.
Hardwick:	Hardwicke is the title of the earldom hereditary in the Yorke family.
Lansdown:	Lansdowne is the title of the marquessate hereditary in the Petty-Fitzmaurice family.
Lindsey:	Lindsay is the title of the earldom hereditary in the Lindesay-Bethune family.
Nairn:	Nairne is the title of the barony hereditary in the Bigham family.
Ronaldsay:	Ronaldshay is the title of the earldom hereditary in the Dundas family.
Roxburgh:	Roxburghe is the title of the dukedom hereditary in the Innes-Ker family.
Scarborough:	Scarbrough is the title of the earldom hereditary in the Lumley family.
Shetland:	Zetland is the title of the marquessate hereditary in the Dundas family.
Winchelsea:	Winchilsea is the title of the earldom hereditary in the Finch Hatton family.

304 Spelling of proper names

The personal usage of the bearer ot the name is to be scrupulously followed:

De Morgan *but:* de la Mare
St John *or:* St. John
Strongitharm *or:* Strong i' th' arm
Macintosh MacIntosh McIntosh
Fitzherbert FitzHerbert

26 AE / OE

In Latin words and in derivatives from them (and from Greek words through the Latin) these letters should be printed separately with no ligature; they are to be set in ligature only in French, Old English and Scandinavian (including Icelandic) words, and in English words derived from them. 305

Caesarea formulae oedema Oedipus Phaedra
but: Ælfric Cædmon hors d'œuvre manœuvre trompe-l'œil

27 -S- OR -Z-?

Many words have two alternative forms of spelling, using either *s* or *z*. Consistency of usage throughout a single work is important. For instance: 306

	rather than:
brazier	brasier
ouzel	ousel
raze	rase

on the other hand:

	rather than:
bombasine	bombazine
hussy	huzzy
totalisator	totalizator
visor	vizor

-ise or -ize? 307
In the large number of words in which these alternative spellings are permissible, many authors prefer '-ize'.

In most of these words, '-ize' is a suffix forming the verb: 308
(a) either from a noun:

apostat(e)-ize	Bowdler bowdlerize
apolog(y)-ize	capital-ize
apostroph(e-)ize	climate acclimat-ize
author-ize	colon(y)-ize

309

critic-ize
crystal(l)-ize
dogma(t)-ize
drama(t)-ize
econom(y)-ize
emphas(is)-ize
eulog(y)-ize
Galvani galvanize
gourmand gormandize
harmon(y)-ize
hypnot(ic)-ize
idol-ize
ion-ize
italic-ize
item-ize
jeopard(y)-ize
Juda(h)-ize
lion-ize
McAdam macadamize
magnet-ize
memor(y)-ize
Mesmer mesmerize
minim(um)-ize
monopol(y)-ize
odour de-odor-ize
organ-ize
oxid(e)-ize
pauper-ize
plagiar(y)-ize
proselyt(e)-ize
revolution-ize
rhapsod(y)-ize
Roman-ize
satir(e)-ize
scandal-ize
scrutin(y)-ize
sermon-ize
soliloqu(y)-ize
standard-ize
symbol-ize
sympath(y)-ize
terror-ize
theor(y)-ize
tyrant tyrannize
vapour vaporize
victim-ize

309 (b) or from an adjective:

American-ize
barbar(ous)-ize
bestial-ize
civil-ize
equal-ize
ethereal-ize
ideal-ize
immortal-ize
immun(e)-ize
laic-ize
Latin-ize
legal-ize
legitim(ate)-ize
liberal-ize
local-ize
material-ize
mobil(e)-ize
modern-ize
moral de-moral-ize
national-ize
natural-ize
neutral-ize
particular-ize
penal-ize
polar-ize
popular-ize
rational-ize
real-ize
secular-ize
sentimental-ize
signal-ize
solemn-ize
steril(e)-ize
systemat(ic)-ize
total-ize
tranquil(l)-ize
universal-ize
visual-ize
vocal-ize
vulgar-ize

and others

Others are words of purely Greek origin: 310

agonize	catechize	hellenize
antagonize	evangelize	ostracize
baptize	exorcize	syllogize

There are, however, a number of words which must *always* 311
end in -ise. The following is a complete list of them:

advertise	emprise	precise
advise	enfranchise	premise
affranchise	enterprise	prise (open)
apprise (inform)	excise	raise
arise	exercise	reprise
braise	expertise	revise
chastise	franchise	rise
circumcise	guise	seise (legal term)
comprise	improvise	supervise
compromise	incise	surmise
concise	mainprise	surprise
demise	merchandise	televise
despise	misadvise	treatise
devise	misprise	upraise
disfranchise	mortise	uprise
disguise	praise	wise

Note: (i) that half the words in this list are compounds of one of the following stems:

-cise (cut)	-prise (take)
-mise (put)	-vise (see)

(ii) that more than a quarter of the words in this list do not end in the normal *ize* sound – e.g. braise, mortise, precise – and so will cause no difficulty in spelling.

-yse 312
Words ending thus must never be spelt with -z- :

analyse catalyse dialyse electrolyse hydrolyse paralyse

28 ANGLICIZATION OF AMERICAN COPY

313 This is not the responsibility of the keyboard operator but of the person whose duty it is to prepare copy for press, either at the publisher's office or in the copy preparation department of the Press.

314 Special regard, in the preparation of copy, must be paid to the difference between American and English usage in capitalization and hyphenation.

315 Most printers are prepared, if requested by the publisher, to carry out simple and obvious changes of spelling: with some words the decision is obvious.

(a) American can be easily changed into English

aluminum	aluminium
caliber	calibre
catalog	catalogue
center	centre
color	colour
defense	defence
dialog	dialogue
fulfillment	fulfilment
gray	grey
honor	honour
humor	humour
jewelry	jewellery
maneuver	manœuvre
marvelous	marvellous
mold	mould
paralyze	paralyse
plow	plough
pretense	pretence
program	programme
skeptical	sceptical
skillful	skilful
smolder	smoulder
theater	theatre
traveling	travelling
willful	wilful
woolen	woollen
worshiped	worshipped

But here is a second list: other words may not be so readily 'naturalized'. 316

(b) American should be changed into English

airplane	aeroplane
alright	all right
anemic	anaemic
anymore	any more
anyplace	anywhere
anytime	at any time
ass	arse
ax	axe
caligraphy	calligraphy
calisthenics	callisthenics
catsup	ketchup
check	cheque
checkered	chequered
coeds	co-eds
cozey, cozy	cosy
curb	kerb
disassociate	dissociate
dove	dived
draftsman	draughtsman
dumfounded	dumbfounded
esthetic	aesthetic
fanatic (adj.)	fanatical
fit (past indicative)	fitted
forever	for ever
hemorrhage	haemorrhage
inclose	enclose
inclosure	enclosure
inlaws	in-laws
insofar	in so far
install	instal
insure	ensure
inthrall	enthral
intrust	entrust
licence (verb)	license
licorice	liquorice
mustache, mustachio	moustache
nonetheless	none the less
onto	on to

peddler	pedlar
percent	per cent
pickaninny	piccaninny
practise (noun)	practice
precipitous	precipitate
sanitarium	sanatorium
someplace	somewhere
specialty	speciality
stanch (adj.)	staunch
tidbit	titbit
tire (noun)	tyre
vender	vendor
yogurt	yoghourt

It becomes clear from the above list that something more than simple spelling is involved: the separation of words, their hyphenation; their status as nouns, adjectives or verbs; their very meaning (*precipitous*, *tire*, *ass*, *insure*, *stanch*).

317 Further problems of anglicization will often arise:

(c) Is American always to be English?

dreamed	dreamt
learned	learnt
smelled	smelt
spelled	spelt
spoiled	spoilt
sunburned	sunburnt
heavenward	heavenwards
inward	inwards
outward	outwards
seaward	seawards
upward	upwards
a half-minute	half a minute
a quarter-mile	a quarter of a mile
a half-century	half a century
a half-hour	half an hour
a half-bottle of beer	half a bottle of beer

(certainly in English usage *a half-bottle of wine* is something quite distinct from *half a bottle of wine*)

all of the day	all the day
aside from	apart from
close to noon	close on noon
in back of the house	behind the house
inside of the shed	inside the shed
named for Kennedy	named after Kennedy
nights	at night
out the window	out of the window
over all of Canada	throughout Canada
spring housecleaning	spring cleaning
whilst	while

Still further, American usage of certain words may be 318
genuinely puzzling to English readers:

(d) Is American correctly rendered by English?

apartment	flat
ashcan	dustbin
baby carriage	pram
baseboards	skirting boards
billboard	poster, hoarding
bobby pins	curlers
cohort	escort, partner
derby	bowler
drapes	blinds, curtains
dresser	dressing table
elevator	lift
fall	autumn
fenders	wings, bumpers
flat	puncture
garbage man	dustman
garters	(sock) suspenders
hallway	corridor, entrance hall
honor guards	guard of honour
hood (of car)	bonnet
intersection	crossroads
janitor	porter
lobby	hall
napery	table linen
overly	excessively, too much
pants	trousers

phonograph	gramophone, record player*
podium	rostrum
sack	handbag
sidewalk	pavement
singlet, undershirt	vest
suspenders	braces
underpants	pants
vest	waistcoat
washrag	face flannel
windshield	windscreen
we visited	we called
I visited with him	I had a chat with him

On the telephone:

we called	we rang
who is this speaking?	who is that speaking?

319 There may be no certain equivalents in English for unknown American words.

(e) Is American translatable into English?

finagle	trick, wangle
hellion	troublemaker
pesthouse	isolation hospital
riffle	turn pages, shuffle

320 These lists illustrate the variety of problems that may be covered by the simple instruction to anglicize. Anglicization is a task that requires the full skill of an editor acting upon explicit decisions as to the public for whom the work is designed and the degree to which it is desired to retain its native American character.

321 Note, finally, that American spelling, vocabulary and phraseology are always to be fully retained:

(i) in American dialogue;
(ii) in passages quoted from American writing;
(iii) in proper names and titles of purely American origin:

---

* *Gramophone*, though widely used, is the proprietary name of one company's product.

American Federation of Labor
Congressional Medal of Honor
Labor Day (first Monday in September)
Library of Congress Catalog
Pearl Harbor
Rockefeller Center

29 TRANSLITERATION

Words of foreign languages that do not use the roman alphabet must be accurately and consistently transliterated, so as to represent as far as possible English consonant and vowel sounds rather than those of the European language prevalent in the country. Russian, Arabic and African words, for example, have often in the past been transliterated into French forms. 322

The following are examples of correct transliteration into English: 323

	not:
Aleksandr Mikhailovich	Alexander Michaelovitch
Aleksei Aleksandrovich	Alexis Alexandrovitch
Aswan	Assouan, Assuan
Asyut	Assiout, Assiut
Bahrain	Bahrein
Beirut	Bairut, Beyrouth
*Chaikovsky	Tschaikowski
Chekhov	Tchekoff
Dukhobor	Doukhobor
Feodor Yakovlevich Aleksyeev	Theodor Jacovlevitch Alexeiev
Harun al-Rashid	Haroun-al-Raschid
Hawash, River	Aouache
Husein	Hussain, Husain
Jibuti	Djibouti

Kamerun	Cameroon
Khartum	Khartoum
*Muhammad	Mahomet
*Razumovsky	Rassoumovski
Sakyamuni	Çakya-mouni
Shaliapin	Chaliapine
Sheherezade	Scheherezade
*Tsarevich	Cesarevitch
Ubangi-Shari-Chad	Oubangui-Chari-Tchad
Ujda	Oudjda
Wadai	Ouadaï
Wagadugu	Ouagadougou
Wazzan	Ouezzane

* Certain less correct forms are hallowed by long usage and should be followed:

the composer Tchaikovsky;

the prophet Mohammed (note that 'Mohamed' is the spelling often preferred by the Arab for his own personal name);

Beethoven's Rasumovsky Quartets;

the Cesarewitch stakes.

324 It should be remembered that faulty transliteration of sacred names or religious formularies can result in a hurtful or even offensive parody of the original.

325 Authorities sometimes differ on standards of transliteration. Consult *The Times Index-Gazetteer of the World*, *Webster's Biographical Dictionary*, *Webster's Geographical Dictionary*. Advice can also be obtained from the embassy of the country in question and from the Royal Geographical Society.

326 Words in a language employing the roman alphabet should, of course, not be transliterated. The name of the famous pianist and one-time President of Poland may be pronounced Paderevsky but it must be spelt Paderewski. The Serbian name Alexander Karageorgevich should be spelt Aleksandar Karadjordjević.

Note that certain newspapers may have their preference, in the spelling of foreign names, for the form that makes for easier reading. For example, the Russian name correctly transliterated Khrushchev was given by the *Daily Mail* and other papers in the more easily readable form: Kruschev. In quotation, this decision must be borne in mind. 327

30 NOTES

Notes should not be used to give essential information which could easily be worked into the text. They should contain only incidental or reference information which would otherwise clutter the text unnecessarily and distract the reader. 328

A note is to be indicated in the text by a superior figure or by one of the conventional marks of reference in order as follows: 329

* † ‡ § || ¶ ** †† ‡‡ §§ etc.

The superior figure or mark should normally be set outside an adjacent mark of punctuation or quotation mark: 330

It was his last work;[3] three weeks later he was dead.

[3] The final chapter was completed on 24 July.

But a superior referring exclusively to a word or phrase immediately preceding it should be set thus: 331

It was a matter of *sauve qui peut**; we all bolted.

* every man for himself

Notes may be either footnotes or endnotes. 332

Notes that are immediately necessary to the reader's understanding of the text may be inserted at the foot of the page. 333

As they will not be numerous, they can be conveniently referred to by the marks of reference shown above:

On his visit to Vlissingen* he met his kinswoman Sophia, Duchess of Brunswick-Lüneburg†.

* Flushing

† later Electress of Hanover

334 Notes that give only references to authorities or are too long to be easily accommodated at the foot of the page may discourage the casual reader, even at a glance at the volume in a bookshop. The best place for them is at the end of the book. They should be referred to in the text by superior figures, easily distinguishable from the marks of reference to the footnotes. Each page, left and right, of these endnotes should have running heads indicating the pages of text to which the notes on that page refer.

335 To place such notes at the end of the book, with this provision of running heads for easy reference, is much preferable to the placing of them at the end of each chapter, where they are difficult to find except with an extra bookmark or a finger kept constantly at the required page.

336 The position of notes at the end of the book has the added advantage that there they can be preceded by an explanatory bibliography or a list of short titles making for conciseness of reference.

337 Footnotes should be set two sizes smaller than the text, and separated from the last line of text by a white space. A rule should not normally be used (i) unless there is at the foot of the text a passage of quoted matter in smaller-size type which the reader might confuse with the small type of the footnote, or (ii) unless footnote matter is carried over from the preceding page.

338 Footnotes must on no account be interrupted by the intervention of a page of illustrations constituting a break in the text.

A footnote should be introduced by a superior figure or mark of reference, indented 1½ ems of the footnote fount and followed by an em space if another footnote begins on the same line. The superior figure must of course be of the same fount as that used in the text. 339

Number the footnotes separately page by page, unless otherwise instructed. 340

Endnotes should be numbered by chapters. They should be introduced by an arabic numeral on the line, followed by full point and en space. They should be set in type one size smaller than the text, as used for quoted matter. 341

Single short footnotes should normally be centred on the measure: 342

* Harrison *Autobiography* Oxford 1934, p. 128

A series of short footnotes (i) either should run on from one another to conserve space, with not less than one em space between them: 343

[1] Harrison, op. cit., p. 134 [2] ibid., pp. 216ff. [3] ibid., pp. 220f.
[4] ibid., pp. 233, 235, 237ff. [5] ibid., pp. 245–8 [6] ibid., p. 263

(ii) or should be ranged left with one another and centred as a whole on the measure: 344

[1] Harrison, op. cit., p. 134
[2] probably a kinsman of the same name
[3] Chetwynd *Life of Wolseley* pp. 56–8
[4] cf. i, 184
[5] Harrison, op. cit., pp. 242ff., 280–93
[6] see p. 22 above
[7] as in 1678

If the footnotes are long and one at least will fill the measure, they should be set to the full measure as separate entries, each beginning with a 1½-ems indent: 345

[1] M'Corquodaile *History of Printing* (Edinburgh 1897), ii, 386–94
[2] ibid., loc. cit.
[3] Alexander Preston *Press and Politics* (Dublin 1913) *passim*
[4] M'Corquodaile, op. cit., i, 27

346 If a note (whether footnote or endnote) begins with any of the abbreviations used for reference, or with a formal expression such as: 'see . . . ', 'quoted from . . . ', followed by a simple reference to the source of the quotation, the initial letter may be set in lower case.

347 Notes giving simply a reference to a book title, author, publisher, date of publication, volume and page, require no full point. Nor do notes giving only an explanatory phrase or reference.

348 Notes, however, consisting of one, or more than one, complete sentence must be normally punctuated, even if that sentence takes the form of a subordinate clause.

349 Notes generally should be as little obtrusive as possible. Avoid capital letters, even in roman numerals. Use abbreviations and contractions as far as possible without loss of clarity or dignity. Keep punctuation to the minimum.

350 The following series of notes, set in the style of endnotes, will serve to illustrate the directions given in the four preceding paragraphs:

1. cited by Cope *The Versatile Victorian* (London 1951), p. 47
2. 22 Geo. III, c. 83
3. e.g. on the death of his aunt, 19 Sept. 1964
4. as, in fact, he had secretly always intended.
5. see vol. i of the present work
6. quoted in *The Times* 16.iv.1966, p. 12, col. 4
7. for the details, see *The Lancet* of that date
8. cf. vol. i, p. 265
9. i.e. all those whose names were on the electoral register
10. popularly nicknamed 'Old Noll'
11. 31 & 32 Vict., c. 122, s. 8
12. e.g. the letter he subsequently wrote during his illness; he had then had time to think things over.
13. see above, p. 10, n. 2
14. but he had not reckoned on her change of fortune.
15. 13 March 1727
16. as reported next day in the *Guardian*

17. 2 Cor. 8:31
18. *Brighton Herald & Hove Chronicle* 28.xi.1914, p. 5, col. 1
19. *a mensa et toro*; which may be translated 'from bed and board'.
20. *Punch* 9.i.1887, p. 42

31 BIBLIOGRAPHIES

The word 'bibliography', strictly speaking, denotes a classified list comprising the principal published, and sometimes unpublished, works dealing with a specific subject. **351**

The word is, however, commonly used of the list, provided by an author, of the various sources of information consulted by him in the preparation of the work to which it is attached. This is the sense in which the word is used here. **352**

The bibliography is normally put at the end of the work. If there are endnotes containing bibliographical references, it will probably be convenient that they should be preceded by the bibliography, which, if lengthy, might include a list of short titles or abbreviations for ease of reference. **353**

If, however, the notes are put earlier, either at the ends of chapters or as footnotes page by page, it may be desirable to place the bibliography at the beginning of the work. It should there follow the other preliminary matter and immediately precede Chapter 1. Sometimes a separate bibliography for each chapter is required, in which case it is again desirable that this should precede the notes, if any, to the chapter. **354**

What the reader looks for in the bibliography is a concise statement of the sources drawn on by the author; together with, perhaps, a short list of books for further reading. An exhaustive account of all the sources consulted is seldom needed. The most useful list is a 'Select Bibliography', with a note explaining its scope and purpose, and with the entries divided into categories. **355**

For instance, the bibliography of a work on international finance in the nineteenth century might have the following categories:

MANUSCRIPT SOURCES

France
Great Britain
United States

PRINTED SOURCES

Newspapers
On the history of banking
On the cotton famine
On Egypt in the nineteenth century

This example is taken from *Bankers and Pashas* by David S. Landes (Heinemann, London 1958). Professor Landes has used the title 'Bibliographical Note' rather than 'Bibliography', and has evaluated and annotated his entries. He refers to library sources and cites a published bibliography on one aspect of his subject. He introduces his printed books section (containing only 16 titles) with the following note:

> Of the large selection of secondary sources used, a number of works are deserving of special mention. Many of these contain bibliographies of their own that should prove helpful to the interested reader.

He has thus not overloaded his own book with unnecessary data, but has given the serious scholar all the information needed to pursue the subject further.

356 Book lists are particularly important in textbooks and educational works, even books for quite young children, and here clarity and ease of reference are essential. Naturally the titles of such lists will be descriptive, e.g. 'Suggestions for further reading'.

357 Within each section of a bibliography, works should be listed in alphabetical order of authors or editors; or, if no author or editor is named, of the organizations sponsoring their publication. Dictionaries, encyclopedias and periodicals may be listed directly under their titles, where a general reference is intended or an unsigned article is referred to.

A bibliographical entry may have the following items, in the order indicated. Recommended typographical style for each item is also given. 358

1. name of author, compiler, editor (followed by 'ed.' in parentheses) or sponsor	caps and small caps, or even small caps (spaced one or two units)
2. title of article, short paper or chapter (e.g. contribution to symposium)	roman upper and lower case, in quotes
3. title of periodical or book	italic upper and lower case
4. name of translator (if any), preceded by 'trans.' or 'tr.'	roman upper and lower case
5. name of editor (if any) responsible for the published form of the work, preceded by 'ed.'	roman upper and lower case
6. the number of volumes (if more than one)	numerals and abbreviations, e.g. '3 vols' (*not* 'three volumes')
7. the number of the edition (other than the first)	roman lower case, using arabic numerals, e.g. '4th edn'
8. the particular volume, part (if any), number and pages referred to	lower case or small caps for volume numbers set in roman numerals, e.g. 'vol. xviii' or 'vol. XVIII' (not 'Vol. XVIII')
9. the name of the series (if any) of which the work forms part	roman upper and lower case
10. the name of the publisher	roman upper and lower case
11. the place of publication	if there is more than one place of publication, these may be separated from one another by an oblique stroke (or solidus)

12. the date of publication (this should be the date of the actual edition consulted)

The minimum entry for a book would consist of items 1, 3, 11 and 12. If the work is still in copyright, item 10 should also be included.

For a signed article in a periodical, the minimum entry would consist of items 1, 2, 3, 8, 11 and 12. This last item may need to include day and month as well as year of publication. The main principle is to give all the details likely to be useful to the person wishing to locate the book or article in question.

359 Accuracy is important: details should be noted from the title page (not the spine, jacket or library binding) of an actual copy of the work, never from memory. In noting the author's name, care should be taken to include all initials and forenames as given on the title page; e.g. M. Penelope Hall (*not* Penelope Hall); John Cowper Powys (*not* J. C. Powys); D. H. Lawrence (*not* David H. Lawrence *or* David Herbert Lawrence). This ensures ease of reference, for example, in library catalogues.

360 The name of the publisher may be shortened, provided that it is easily identifiable: e.g. Faber (for Faber and Faber); Heinemann Educational (for Heinemann Educational Books Ltd); Longmans (for Longmans, Green & Co.); Methuen (for Methuen & Co. Ltd).

361 It is desirable to use as few marks of punctuation as possible in bibliographical entries, and to omit them altogether when their function is performed by a change in the style of type used. Thus, no punctuation is necessary between author and title, or between place and year of publication, or at the end of the entry. Some specimen entries using different styles are given below.

[a] books

MATTHEW PRIOR *Poems on Several Occasions* 2 vols, Berwick 1766 **362**

The name of the printer-bookseller, R. Taylor, might have been included in a specialist bibliography.

DONALD DAVIE (ed.) *The Late Augustans: longer poems of the later eighteenth century* The Poetry Bookshelf, general editor James Reeves (Heinemann, London 1958) **363**

Note that the sub-title of the work has been separated from the main title by a colon. The name of the series in which this selection appears (The Poetry Bookshelf) would be useful for most readers.

DONALD A. STAUFFER *The Nature of Poetry* The Norton Library (paperback), Norton, New York 1946 **364**

A work of popularization: it is therefore relevant to know that this volume is in a paperback series.

RAINER MARIA RILKE *Duino Elegies*: the German text, with an English translation, introduction and commentary by J. B. Leishman and Stephen Spender; The Hogarth Press, London 1952 **365**

A shorter entry than this would be insufficient to explain the contents of the book. Note the use of the colon to introduce the explanation.

The above entries illustrate some possible styles of punctuation where it is necessary to separate publication details from title etc. It is neat to enclose the publication details in parentheses (**363**); on the other hand, parentheses may be useful for other purposes (as in **364**). In **365**, a semicolon has been used to separate off the publication details, but a comma (see **364**) or a colon (see **367–9**) is to be preferred. **366**

367 NORMAN COHN *The Pursuit of the Millennium* (a history of popular religious and social movements in Europe from the eleventh to the sixteenth century): Secker & Warburg, London 1957

In this entry the colon used to separate the publication details from the rest may not appear necessary because of the adjacent parenthesis, but subsequent entries might well need a mark of punctuation at this point (see **368**), and consistency is desirable.

368 Page numbers are useful where an article or chapter in a symposium is referred to. In the entry below, the word 'in' seems necessary to link the article with the book title, which should be *preceded* by the editor's name. For example, a chapter on the freedom of the press may well form part of a work on the wider subject of human rights. A bibliography on the freedom of the press might include the following:

ARMAND GASPARD 'International Action to Preserve Press Freedom', in EVAN LUARD (ed.) *The International Protection of Human Rights* pp. 183–209: Thames and Hudson, London 1967

369 whereas in a bibliography on human rights the entry would read:

EVAN LUARD (ed.) *The International Protection of Human Rights*: Thames and Hudson, London 1967

370 It is only in bibliographies heavily loaded with detail or annotation that more profuse punctuation is necessary. A bibliography containing many entries of the complexity of the following would need care in the styling of punctuation:

OSWALD SPENGLER *The Decline of the West* [*Der Untergang des Abendlandes*, revised edition 1922] trans. Charles Francis Atkinson: vol. i *Form and Actuality* [*Gestalt und Wirklichkeit*]; vol. ii *Perspectives of World-History* [*Welthistorische Perspektiven*]: Allen & Unwin, London n.d. (translator's prefaces January 1926 and July 1928)

[b] periodicals

Some specimen entries for articles in periodicals are given below.

GERALD SEAMAN 'Amateur Music-Making in Russia' *Music and Letters* (ed. J. A. Westrup) vol. 47, no. 3, pp. 249–59, Oxford University Press, London, July 1966 **371**

Note that here it is important to state the place of publication. The *editorial offices* of this journal are in Oxford, but it is *published* by the Music Department of the Oxford University Press in London. The style of the numerals for volume and number (arabic) follows that used by the journal itself. It is not essential to give the editor's name, but it may well be of interest.

FELIX HOERBURGER 'Folk Dance Survey' (report to the Seventeenth Annual Conference of the International Folk Music Council) *Journal of the International Folk Music Council* vol. xviii, part 1, pp. 7–8: W. Heffer & Sons Ltd, Cambridge, England, March 1965 **372**

Here the explanation in parentheses would normally be of interest. Also it is necessary, when referring to an international journal, to state clearly the place of publication. 'England' is required here in order to distinguish Cambridge, England, from Cambridge, Massachusetts.

ERNŐ LENDVAI 'Duality and Synthesis in the Music of Béla Bartók' *The New Hungarian Quarterly* ed. Iván Boldizsár, vol. iii, no. 7, pp. 91–114: Corvina Press, Budapest, July–September 1962 **373**

In **371** the name of the editor of the journal was given in parentheses; here it is separated by a comma from the details which follow. These are two possible styles among several.

LAURENCE MARTIN 'If Arabs had Wings' *Spectator* vol. 219, no. 7272, p. 564: London, Friday 10 November 1967 **374**

It would here be superfluous to state the publisher (The Spectator Ltd), but it might well be considered insular of an

English scholar to omit the place of publication, especially in a bibliography on an international topic.

375 Page references should always be given in this type of entry, as they facilitate reference to bound volumes.

376 Further illustrations of the points discussed above will be found in Section 1 of this book, paragraphs **1** to **8**. The style used there for punctuation and typography is that especially recommended. See also **397**.

377 Finally, however, it must be remembered, whatever style is chosen, that in a bibliography consistency and clarity are of the first importance.

Full bibliographical descriptions (of the kind required by professional librarians and bibliographers) lie outside the scope of this book. For a specimen typographical styling of such a description see Oliver Simon's *Introduction to Typography* rev. edn (Faber, London 1963), p. 101.

32 REFERENCES

378 References to authorities and sources for quotations may be given either in footnotes to the page or in endnotes set preferably at the end of the work. If they are important to the student, but are likely to distract rather than interest the general reader, they are better printed as endnotes. Reference to endnotes should be made easy by the provision of running heads on both left and right pages giving the pages of text they refer to (see **334**).

379 References should be kept to the minimum length required to enable the reader to find the source of the information with ease. Their constituent parts should be the same as those of bibliographical entries: the minimum details necessary for the first reference to a work will consist of the author's name, the title of the work quoted, and the place and date of publication; only details already given in the text itself will be omitted. In addition, the particular page or

pages referred to will usually be given; other information will be given as required, in the order already suggested (see **358**). The author's name, however, will be set in upper and lower case, since small capitals, as suggested above in **358**, would appear somewhat heavy in a note.

[1] Arthur Koestler *The Sleepwalkers: a history of man's changing vision of the Universe* (Hutchinson, London 1959), pp. 384–8 **380**

Or if the author's name had already been given in the text, this would be omitted in the note.

Subsequent reference to the same work may be shortened by giving the author's surname alone, shortening the title of the work, and omitting the details of publication: **381**

[1] Koestler *The Sleepwalkers* p. 389

Some authors may prefer maximum conciseness, when a reference is repeated, thus: **382**

[1] Koestler, p. 389

but this shortened form can, of course, be used only if no reference is made to any other work by this author.

References to articles in periodicals should follow the same style: **383**

[1] Kenneth Watson, 'A Reading of *Lord of the Flies*', *English* vol. xv, no. 85 (Oxford, Spring 1964), pp. 2ff.

In a second, shortened reference the title of the article may well be repeated, rather than the volume, number, etc. of the periodical, so long as the original entry is within a page or two: **384**

[1] Watson, 'A Reading of *Lord of the Flies*', p. 4

But if the name of the periodical can be easily shortened, and a list of abbreviations is given in the bibliography for reference, the shortened form may be used: **385**

first reference

[1] J. M. Greene, 'Consequences of automation' *English Labour Review* vol. ix, no. 3 (Sept. 1952), pp. 432ff.

second reference

[1] Greene *E.L.R.* vol. ix, p. 435

third reference

[1] Greene, op. cit., p. 436

386 The term 'op. cit.' (*opere citato*, 'in the work cited') is used to refer back to a work of which bibliographical details have already been given. Like shortened titles, it must be used with care. The reader must be left in no doubt which work is being referred to, and in practice this normally means that the term should be used only on the same page as the original reference (or at farthest on the page facing it). Since pagination can be decided only at the stage when the printer is making up the pages – an operation over which author or editor rarely has control – it is on the whole best to avoid the term, at least in footnotes. For any saving of typesetting effected by its use is often cancelled out by the resetting necessitated when the book is paged.

In endnotes, on the other hand, the use of 'op. cit.' has the merit of saving space and time.

387 The term 'loc. cit.' (*loco citato*, 'in the place cited') is to be used with even greater care. It should refer back only to the actual page in the reference cited earlier.

388 The terms 'id.' (*idem*, 'the same person') and 'ibid.' (*ibidem*, 'in the same place') are to be carefully distinguished. In bibliographical references the meaning of 'id.' is 'the same author'; the meaning of 'ibid.' is 'the same author and title'.

389 The use of 'id.' is commonly neglected in favour of 'ibid.':

[1] Charles Dickens *Oliver Twist* ch. 4

[2] ibid., *Nicholas Nickleby* ch. 2 **[wrong]**

footnote 2 is incorrect; it should read:

[2] id., *Nicholas Nickleby* ch. 2

Moreover, 'ibid.' is often used wrongly instead of 'op. cit.' or 'loc. cit.', thus: 390

[1] Charles Dickens *Oliver Twist* ch. 4

[2] Dickens, ibid., ch. 5 **[wrong]**

footnote 2 is incorrect; it should read:

[2] ibid., ch. 5

But if another note has intervened between the former and latter references to *Oliver Twist*, the notes should then read as follows: 391

[1] Charles Dickens *Oliver Twist* ch. 4

[2] A similar picture of slum conditions is given by Booth.

[3] Dickens, op. cit., ch. 5

If reference is made to a particular passage in a book, and it is desired to refer to the same passage in the following note, it is not enough to use 'ibid.' alone. The notes should read as follows: 392

[1] Charles Dickens *Oliver Twist* ed. 1839, p. 25

[2] ibid., loc. cit.

The remarks above on these important distinctions are not to be taken as recommending the use of Latin references. They are, however, widely used in works of scholarship, and must therefore be understood and used correctly. 393

English references are on the whole to be preferred to Latin. It is clearer and shorter to write 'see above' and 'see below' than '*vide supra*' and '*vide infra*'; again, 'f.' ('and the following page') and 'ff.' ('and the following [two or more] pages') are preferable to 'sq.' and 'sqq.' 394

References to plays, poetry, classical and standard works usually omit shortened forms for 'act', 'scene', 'canto', 'book', 'line', etc.: 395

Congreve *The Way of the World* II, iv

Homer *Iliad* xxiii, 204

Milton *Paradise Lost* iv, 161

Shakespeare *All's Well That Ends Well* III, iv, 18
2 Henry IV II, iii, 27

Shelley *The Cenci* v, iv, 158

Spenser *The Faerie Queene* II, XII, lxxv

Virgil *Aeneid* vi, 352

Note that, where possible without loss of clarity, capital letters are lowered to small capitals.

396 For the sake of clarity it is best not to omit 'p.' and 'vol.', except where the conventions are clearly defined (as in writing for a specialist readership).

397 Some publishers, particularly of learned and scientific journals, print volume numbers in bold type, thus:

B. J. N. Galliers, 'Baptism in the Writings of John Wesley', *Proceedings of the Wesley Historical Society* **32** (1959–69), 121–4

This practice is not recommended in continuous text matter, or even footnotes, for aesthetic reasons – numbers in bold type, scattered here and there in the text, look unattractive – but it may be useful in a bibliography or in endnotes.

398 The following short list of specimen notes of reference may serve to illustrate the principles set out in this section:

[1] T. P. Courtenay *Memoirs of the Life, Works and Correspondence of Sir William Temple Bart.* 2 vols (London 1836), vol. i, pp. 285–6

[2] ibid., p. 287

[3] D. E. Littlewood, 'On the number of terms in a simple algebraic form' *Proc. Camb. Phil. Soc.* vol. 38 (1942), pp. 304–6

[4] 'Acoustics' *Harvard Dict. of Music* (Harvard 1944), pp. 11ff.

[5] Gustave Reese *Music in the Middle Ages* (Norton, New York 1940), p. 369

[6] id. *Music in the Renaissance* (Dent, London 1954), p. 12f.

[7] George Makins *Elementary Physiology* 25th edn (Macdonald, Cambridge 1947), ch. xxii, p. 456

[8] Walther Köhler *Zwingli und Luther* vol. i (Leipzig 1924), p. 86; vol. ii, ed. Kohlmeyer–Bornkamm (Gütersloh 1953), p. 127

33 SCRIPTURE REFERENCES

Arabic numerals should be used. 399
Chapter should be separated from verse by a colon.
Verses should be separated from one another by a comma.
Chapters of the same book (whether followed by a verse or not) should be separated from one another by a semicolon.
Extent of verses should be indicated by an en rule.
In numbers giving extent of verses, the tens figure should always be given, being repeated if necessary.
Extent of chapters (whether followed by verses or not) should be indicated by an em rule.

2 Kings 18:11–13

Ezra 3:23–25

2 Cor. 4:6; 7:3, 10, 12

Rev. 5:10—17:4

Mark 3:19—4:34; Matthew 12:22–32, 46–50; Luke 11:14–26; 8:19–21, 4–15

John 14—15

Mark 7:1—8:26; Matthew 15:1—16:12

Luke 9:51–56; 10:1–16, 21–24; 12; 13:31–35; John 7:11–53; 8:12–59

If the version of the Bible quoted is to be indicated, small capitals should be used: 400

Exod. 20:1 RV

1 Sam. 5:6 RSV

Phil. 2:7—3:10 NEB

Philem. 4 JB

Titles of Scriptural books may be abbreviated in such references, but they are not to be abbreviated in the main text: 401

'Judge not, that ye be not judged' (Matt. 7:1 AV).

but: It is in Matthew 7:1 AV that the famous words are found: 'Judge not, that ye be not judged.'

402 Titles mentioned in the text without reference to chapter and verse may need to be italicized, as normal book titles are, for the sake of clarity:

> Apart from the light thrown on this matter by *Revelation*, we should be left in considerable uncertainty.
>
> *John* [i.e. the Gospel, not the apostle] appears to know nothing of the virgin birth.

34 PAGINATION

403 The prelims should normally be numbered separately from the text, in lower-case roman numerals; half-title, title-page, imprint page and any blank pages bear no folio numbers.

404 Arabic numerals, beginning with 1, start from the first page of the text. If the text begins with a part title backed by a blank, the folio on the first page of the first chapter will be 3.

405 In works of fiction particularly, prelims may be numbered continuously with the text.

406 Lower-case roman numerals should not be followed with arabic numerals as continuing the same series. If prelims are not to be numbered separately they should be numbered in arabic numerals.

407 Foot folios are to be omitted from full-page illustrations and from the last page of the text.

408 Pages on which chapters begin should bear no head folios. If the list of contents gives their page numbers, foot folios should be inserted on these pages, perhaps in a smaller size. Fount for these smaller numbers must be chosen carefully.

35 HEADLINES

409 Normally, running headlines on the left-hand pages give the title of the book; those on the right-hand pages give the title of the chapter. It may occasionally be useful, however, especially in textbooks, to use the left-hand headline for

the chapter title and the right-hand headline to summarize the contents of the two pages.

No headline is printed on a short page beginning a new chapter. 410

If prelims are numbered separately, and any section – Contents, Illustrations, Glossary, Preface, etc. – occupies more than one page, the running heads should consist of the title of that section on both left- and right-hand pages. 411

Similarly, the running heads for endmatter – Appendixes, Bibliography, Notes, List of Symbols and Abbreviations, Glossary, Index, etc. – should consist of the title of each section on both left- and right-hand pages. This style will, of course, be essential if the running heads of the notes indicate the pages of text to which they refer. 412

36 BREAK-LINES

The last line of a paragraph should contain not fewer than four characters. 413

The first line of a new page should be of full length. An exception to this rule has to be allowed only in dialogue. 414

37 DIVISION OF WORDS

Words must inevitably sometimes be broken at the end of the line. The rule should be to divide words as seldom as possible, while avoiding any conspicuously wide or close spacing between words. Occasionally an unorthodox division may be preferable to spacing so wide or so crowded as to be unsightly. 415

A word should not be divided at the bottom of a left-hand page, unless this is quite unavoidable. A word should on no account be divided if the facing right-hand page consists of tabular matter or is taken up with illustrations, and therefore constitutes an interruption in the text. 416

417 A word should never be divided:

(a) at the bottom of a right-hand page;
(b) above a block in the text.

418 Avoid hyphens at the end of more than two successive lines.

419 Do not divide the suffixes:

–able –ible

nor the endings:

–cial –cian –cious –sion –tial –tion –tious

All these can be carried over to the next line:

	not:
irreplace-able	irreplacea-ble
digest-ible	digesti-ble
spe-cial	spec-ial
patri-cian	patric-ian
substan-tial	substant-ial
conten-tious	content-ious

420 Letters pronounced closely together must not be divided:

ae ou aw ow ch sh ph qu cl sl gr tr st sp

	not:
mach-inery, machin-ery	mac-hinery
ac-claim	acc-laim
circum-spect	circums-pect
instruc-tive	ins-tructive, inst-ructive
tele-gram	teleg-ram

Never divide:

ll in Welsh words
ch, *ll* in Spanish words
ij in Dutch words

Three consecutive consonants should be divided so as not to separate the pair which can be easily pronounced together: **421**

	not:
unim-pressed	unimp-ressed
dis-criminate	disc-riminate

Wherever possible, divide a word in such a way that the former part suggests the latter: **422**

	rather than:
fool-ishness	foo-lishness
reinstate-ment	rein-statement
learn-ing	lear-ning
corru-gated, corrug-ated	cor-rugated
starva-tion	star-vation

It is especially important to ensure that a word-division does not suggest a totally different word: **423**

	not:
re-adjust	read-just
re-alignment	real-ignment
re-allocation	real-location
re-ignited	reign-ited
re-infuse	rein-fuse
re-insert	rein-sert
re-publication	republic-ation
re-state	rest-ate

This division will guard against the impression at first sight that the words are compounds of *read*, *real*, *reign*, *rein*, *republic*, *rest*, respectively.

As a general rule, avoid two-letter divisions, taking care especially not to separate prefixes such as: **424**

be- de- en- in- un-
and the suffix -er or the ending -ed

425 A consonant between two vowels should usually be kept with the second vowel, since it is easier to pronounce a consonant before than after a vowel:

politi-cal   disso-nance

426 An *r* between two vowels is, however, an exception, since it modifies the sound of the preceding vowel, and should therefore be associated with it:

cur-ate   ser-ial   bur-ial

But to this rule also there are exceptions:

accu-rate   obdu-rate

427 Do not divide expressions of date or of time by the clock.

428 Avoid, wherever in any way possible, dividing proper nouns (though admittedly *Nebuchadnezzar* or *Antananarivo* may prove unwieldy).

429 Do not divide house numbers from street names.

430 Do not divide words of one syllable, even in their two-syllable plural forms:

hinges   hutches   matches

431 Divide present participles or gerunds, if necessary, before the ending *-ing*, which may be carried over. If the consonant before *-ing* has been doubled to form the participle or gerund, carry over the second of the two consonants, but not otherwise:

	but:
travel-ling	swell-ing
prefer-ring	err-ing

Note also such divisions as:

batt-ling   troub-ling   puzz-ling

432 Divide compound words into their original elements:

pick-pocket   under-graduate

Avoid adding a further division to words already hyphenated: 433

ab-sent-minded fellow-country-man
co-opera-tive un-Ameri-can
for artillery-observa-tion work

It should be added that strict observance of any of the foregoing rules may well be impossible when working to narrow measures where close and even spacing is asked for. 434

38 INDEXES

Nearly every work of non-fiction should be provided with an index, and many a work of fiction would be the better for one. There are, in fact, few works of which it can be said that an index adds nothing to the reader's advantage or interest. The quick consultation of an index in a bookshop will often decide a hesitant buyer to make a purchase. An index will no less often enable the reader to renew his pleasure in certain passages, or even to settle down to the re-reading of a work he has once enjoyed. 435

The omission of an index from a book or periodical dealing with biography, travel, history, or research of any kind is, of course, a crime against the serious reader; but it is a crime too often committed. 436

Such outsize works of fiction as *The Forsyte Saga* or *War and Peace* would benefit considerably by the inclusion of an index; the same is true of novels approaching more normal length, such as *Dombey and Son* or *Tom Jones*. 437

Publishers' contracts usually stipulate that the provision of the index, if any, shall be the responsibility of the author; since the author is best acquainted with the leading topics of the work and their relative importance, he is no doubt the ideal person for the job. But indexing is skilled work, it takes time, and it is not to be lightly undertaken; it may well be worth while engaging a professional indexer to do it. 438

The Society of Indexers* can supply the names of indexers competent to handle material on a variety of subjects.

439 Indexing should not be left to the eleventh hour: the publisher's production schedule must allow adequate time for the index to be compiled. Indexers should be supplied with their material – in the form of typescript or galley proofs – at as early a stage as possible. The subsequent adjustment of page references, at the final page-proof stage, does not involve much time or difficulty. Account must be taken of any last-minute corrections in proof which may affect the index.

440 The length of indexes varies greatly. They are usually set in two columns to the page, though a large page may take three columns. An average-size index to a book of the normal length of 256 pages will occupy about 8 pages (16 columns), though the index of a historical work of 500 pages may well run to as much as 25 pages (50 columns): one page of index to 20 of text. A. J. P. Taylor's *English History 1914–1945* (Oxford University Press, London 1965), a book of 601 pages, carries an index of 51 pages (102 columns): one page of index to 12 of text. The admirably full index to *Miscellany-at-Law* by R. E. Megarry Q.C. (Stevens & Sons, London 1955) occupies 37 pages (74 columns) to 365 pages of text: a ratio of about 1:10 pages. An outstanding example of an index-concordance is to be found in volume xxxix of *Works of John Ruskin* Library Edition, edited by E. T. Cook and Alexander Wedderburn (London 1903–12). It consists of 689 pages, contains nearly 25,000 titles, and gives more than 150,000 references.

441 The compiler of any substantial index (say, of eight pages or more) should, if other than the author, have the right to be given explicit credit for the work, just as translators and illustrators are named. This is most appropriately done under the title of the index:

INDEX

COMPILED BY A.N. OTHER

---

* Hon. Secretary: c/o Barclays Bank Ltd, 1 Pall Mall East, London S.W.1

There is seldom need for more than one index. Persons, places, titles of works referred to, may all be classified as subjects. If Greek quotations or Scriptural references, for example, are given separate indexes to themselves, on account of alphabetical difficulties, this fact should be noted at the head of the main index. **442**

Symbols and isolated entries in non-roman script may be incorporated in a general index. **443**

Everything in the work may be indexed, and usually should be: text, footnotes, endnotes, preliminary matter, appendixes, even illustrations conveying some detailed information. The reader may wish to refer to any of this matter. **444**

Advertisements – in such works as a Town Guide, a Dog Breeder's Year Book, or a technical periodical – should be indexed separately, as they are in no sense part of the author's work. **445**

In considering the type of index required, the indexer should put himself in the position of the reader. If the subject is a technical one, for instance, he might consider the possibility of a combined index and glossary. **446**

The indexer must imagine what subjects a user of the book would be likely to look up, what key-words spring at once to mind, what names in the book are particularly important. **447**

He should aim at simplicity in his choice of key-words: **448**

pensions	**not:** superannuation
death	**not:** mortality

But he should also bear in mind those readers who might look for the subject under a different heading. Where necessary, he will cross-reference, thus: **449**

agriculture: *see* farming

450 The actual work of compilation requires a set of cards or pieces of stiff paper, one for each entry, which can finally be shuffled into alphabetical order.

451 The position of the index is usually (at least in English-speaking countries) at the end of the work; it may sometimes, however, be more convenient, e.g. in periodicals, to place it with the preliminary pages. The position of the index should always be shown in the list of contents.

452 Preliminary notes at the head of the index should indicate the principles on which it has been compiled: the method of alphabetical arrangement; whether any of the references are to columns, paragraphs, sections or divisions of the book other than pages; the significance of bold or other special type used in the index; whether there is a second or third index devoted to special subjects; and so on.

453 Alphabetical arrangement should normally be word-by-word rather than letter-by-letter. Definite and indefinite articles should be avoided; if essential, they should be placed at the end of the entry. For example:

	not:
music	music
music-cases	musicality
music copying	*The Musical Times*
music engraving	music-cases
Musical Times, The	music copying
musicality	music engraving
musicology	musicology

454 A single letter should be regarded as a word; symbols, including numerals, should be indexed as if spelt out, and non-roman alphabets as if transliterated. For example:

C
C major
chalumeau register
χρόαι (*chroai*)
Couperin, François
courante

< (*crescendo*)
crooks
cuivré
cymbals

double bass

⊓ (downbow)

δράγμα (*dragma*)
duple time
dynamic marks

'1812' Overture
embouchure
equal temperament

Two items in the above example might appear in a glossarial 455
index as follows:

< (*crescendo*): growing louder 61
cuivré: a 'brassy' sound 44

Prefixes such as 'Mc' should be treated as if spelt out in full: 456

McEwen, B. D.
MacEwen, R. T.
Macey, S. L.
Macgregor, M. O.
Mack-Smith, S. T.
M'Pherson, H.
Madden, E. M.

Indexes of any complexity will need to have subsidiary 457
entries as well as main entries, and it is essential that these should be clearly arranged. According to the nature of the subject matter, the arrangement of subentries may be alphabetical, chronological, or by page references, or in some other recognized logical or systematic order; the system used should be specified in the preliminary note.

Punctuation must be exact, if ambiguity is to be avoided. 458

A main entry which has no page references of its own should 459
be followed by a colon to introduce the subsequent subentries.

460 Subentries which are run on should be separated by semi-colons.

461 No comma is needed before the first page reference of each entry; but plenty of space should be allowed, to ensure clarity.

books: design of 14–16; indexing of *foreword*, 7, 13; paper for 8, 9; type faces for 20–4

462 No final mark of punctuation is necessary; full points should be avoided throughout (except after abbreviations).

463 If sub-subentries are required, it may be clearer (if space is available) to set each subentry (indented) on a new line. In this case no colon is necessary after the main entry:

books
design of: in U.K. 16–18; in U.S.A. 24–6; in U.S.S.R. 28–30
indexing of *foreword*, 7, 13
paper for: antique laid 8; antique wove 8; machine finished 9; coated 9
typefaces for: linotype 20–1; monotype 23–4

464 For maximum clarity sub-subentries might also be set line by line, indented below the subentries. When subentries extend from one column to the next, the main entry – and, if necessary, any subentry – should be repeated at the top of the next column, with the word 'continued' (perhaps contracted thus: *contd*) added in italic and enclosed in parentheses.

465 The size of type used for the index is normally smaller than that used in the text, and will often be the same size as the footnotes. It must be chosen to suit the character and length of the index and the number of pages available for it. It should in any case be easily legible, and not smaller than 7-point.

466 The initial letter of entries should not be capitalized (except where normally required).

Blocks of entries under successive letters of the alphabet should be separated from one another by a good space, without further typographical distinction. The practice of using small capitals for the first entry of a new block is by no means always convenient, as this entry may well be a book title requiring to be set in italic. 467

Italic is often required for book titles and similar entries; it is therefore best to avoid other use of italic, except for cross-references such as *see*, *see also*, which are thus distinguished from actual entries. 468

In a complex index it may be thought desirable to set the most important page-reference figures in bold type. Arabic numerals in italic may be used for reference to text illustrations, and roman numerals (lower case or small caps) for plates. Whatever system is used should be explained in the preliminary note. 469

If text pages carry more than one column, a suitable reference system should be devised and similarly explained: for example, a, b, c, for column 1, column 2, column 3: 470

typefaces for: linotype 20a, 21b; monotype 23–4; *see also* filmsetting

Further illustration of the points discussed above will be found in the index to this book.

39 PREPARATION OF MANUSCRIPTS

Time spent by authors and editors on the careful preparation of manuscripts is never wasted, since corrections become more expensive to make as production progresses. New processes such as filmsetting require even more meticulous copy preparation than is required for movable type processes. 471

All manuscripts should be typed, unless this is impossible owing to the nature of the material, as for instance in the 472 case of some advanced mathematical works. The wise author makes at least three copies: the top copy to send to his publisher, the second to retain for reference, and the third as a spare, in case the first one should go astray or the publisher should require a duplicate (e.g. for selling foreign rights or going forward with the jacket design).

473 If the material is handwritten, acceptable carbon copies can be made by the use of a ball-point pen; alternatively, photocopies may be made at a later stage.

474 Unique documents, especially handwritten manuscripts, should always be registered in transit.

475 Manuscripts should be typed in double spacing, on one side only of good-quality quarto paper, with generous margins. Quotations of five lines or more should be typed in single spacing, indented. Footnotes should also be in single spacing. It is easier for the publisher if each note is typed not at the foot of the page but immediately below the line it refers to, and separated from the text above and below by rules.

476 Pages should be numbered throughout, at the upper right-hand corner. Once this numbering has been done, the pages should remain in place. Any deleted matter should be crossed through firmly; even if the whole of a page is deleted, that page should not be removed, or it may be thought to have been lost or mislaid.

477 Substantial additions to the manuscript should be inserted on separate sheets marked, for example, '91a', '91b', etc.

478 Any small manuscript alterations to the text should be clearly written in ink: on a script which has been typed in double spacing this is easily done between the lines. The margins should be left clean as far as possible for typographical instructions to the printer.

Before being sent to the printer, the script should include all preliminary matter, some of which will be added by the publisher. According to the nature of the work, this may need to comprise, though not necessarily in the precise order shown below, some or all of the following: 479

HALF-TITLE	title of book; sometimes 'blurb'
VERSO OF HALF-TITLE	list of works by the same author; books in the same series
TITLE-PAGE	title of book; name of author, editor, translator, illustrator, etc.; name of publisher; place of publication; sometimes date
VERSO OF TITLE-PAGE	date; copyright notice; Library of Congress catalog card number; Standard Book Number (SBN); publisher's and printer's imprints

DEDICATION

LIST OF CONTENTS

LIST OF ILLUSTRATIONS (PLATES)

LIST OF DIAGRAMS, MAPS, ETC.

FOREWORD OR PREFACE

ACKNOWLEDGEMENTS

INTRODUCTION

LIST OF ABBREVIATIONS

LIST OF WORKS CITED

EDITORIAL NOTE

It is best to number these preliminary pages ('prelims') separately in lower-case roman numerals (both in typescript and in proof), since this allows for flexibility in make-up: it is thus possible to adjust the total number of pages, if necessary in the interests of economical production. 480

All endmatter except the index (which can only be completed at final page-proof stage) should also be included: appendixes, bibliography, endnotes, glossary. 481

482 If the book is to be made up straight into pages, with no intervening galley-proof stage, the running headlines will also need to be specified: normally these consist of the book title on the left-hand page and the chapter title on the right-hand page. But if either is unduly long, acceptable short forms must be found.

483 Typographical marks should not be made by the author on his own manuscript, except in consultation with the publisher. The author's responsibility is to ensure that his system of sections and sub-sections is logical and consistent, and that headings follow a uniform pattern. They should be typed in roman upper and lower case: the publisher's staff will then decide on type of the appropriate weight for them – whether capitals, small capitals, bold, or italic. If the copy is consistent and the system of headings clear, it is not usually necessary to mark typographical style for more than the first few pages: this should be a matter of collaboration between the publisher's editorial and production departments, in consultation with the printer.

484 If the author wishes to make special use of italic or bold type in the text itself – for instance, in a highly technical work – he should consult the publisher before marking his script. For ordinary use of italic (indicated in typescript by single underlining) see Section 18.

485 It is important that any cross-references needed should be inserted in the text at manuscript stage; to do this later may involve the re-setting of several lines of type. Cross-references should take the form, 'see p. oo', 'see also chapter 6, p. oo', etc., thus leaving room for the page numbers to be inserted.

486 Index copy should, if time allows, be typed in the same way as the manuscript itself. If time is short, however, most publishers and printers will accept index copy in the form of numbered cards or slips, provided that these are legible and consistent.

Before preparing illustrations an author should consult his publisher: the production process to be used will determine his method of preparation. In general, text diagrams should be numbered and their position indicated, but the drawings themselves (or roughs for an artist to work from) should be supplied on separate sheets. Photographs etc. to be reproduced as separate plates should also be numbered (lightly in pencil on the back) and a list of captions supplied. Glossy prints should be submitted, and care taken not to damage them with paper clips or to write on the back with ball-point pen. **487**

The pages of a typescript should be tied together loosely in appropriate sections with tape so that they can be opened out flat. Illustrations should be suitably protected in a separate folder. **488**

A system of different coloured inks may be used for editorial amendments which might also carry through to the stage of proof correction: for instance, green for publisher's editor, blue for printer's reader, and red for author. **489**

Editorial alterations of any consequence should be agreed with the author before the manuscript is finally sent to the printer. **490**

Manuscript instructions from publisher to printer on the typescript should be ringed round, to distinguish them from alterations to the text itself. Purely typographical instructions are best made in pencil. The conventions and signs used for these are the same as for proof correction (see Section 40). **491**

40 CORRECTION OF PROOFS

If the manuscript has been carefully prepared, correction of proofs should amount to no more than rectification of printer's errors, insertion of any page references, and minor adjustment of spacing, etc. Authors should not view the appearance of galley proofs (still less of page proofs) as an opportunity to rewrite their books. Since they may be **492** charged by publishers for excess corrections it is in their own interests to make sure that their original manuscripts are in final form.

493 At the same time it is often only at the proof stage that minor inaccuracies come to light: this is the last opportunity to put them right, if the indignity of an errata slip is to be avoided. The indexer in particular is likely to spot any inconsistencies in the spelling of names or quotation of dates, and he should always be asked to make a note of these, and of any other necessary corrections. The printer's reader too has the advantage of bringing a fresh mind to bear on a subject perhaps by now over-familiar to author and editor. Any queries from him should be carefully considered: if his suggestions are not accepted they should simply be struck through and no offence will be taken.

494 If a system of different coloured inks for printer's, editor's, and author's corrections is adopted (as suggested above, **489**), much unnecessary correspondence is avoided. A further refinement of such a system appreciated by printers is for editor and author to use yet another colour for marking corrections of actual printer's errors – deviation from the copy as submitted – as opposed to their own second thoughts. This helps the printer in his accounting: he will not charge his customer for errors made by his own compositors. Naturally any such system should be clarified in advance with all concerned.

495 The printer will submit a 'marked set' of proofs together with as many spares as the publisher requests. This marked set is precious and should not be used for rough working. Publishers usually supply authors with a duplicate set which can be used for this purpose, and also retained for reference. The publisher's editor will normally collate any other corrections (made by the indexer, the publisher's proof-reader, or perhaps an 'outside' specialist reader in the case of a technical work) on the marked set and settle any final queries with the author. The production staff will also wish to check that design instructions have been followed and that no typographical defects remain uncorrected before returning the proof, passed for press, to the printer. The retention of a 'dummy' reference set (with all corrections marked) in the publisher's office is highly desirable.

The main principle in proof correction is to keep alterations 496
to the minimum and ensure absolute clarity. If new material *must* be inserted, every effort should be made to delete or condense other material to make room for it. This sometimes involves the laborious counting of letters and spaces, but is much less costly than upsetting a number of lines, or worse, paragraphs, or worse still, pages. If any matter has to be repaged this will not only be expensive in itself, but may also affect the contents list, illustrations, notes, and index. Similarly, deleted material should be compensated for, if at all possible.

Handwriting should be unmistakably clear: if there is any 497
possibility of error (in reading, for instance, 'lovesome' for 'lonesome') the ambiguous word or phrase should be repeated in block capitals, ringed, in the outer margin. Any substantial additions should be typed in full.

Corrections should be marked in the margin of the proof, 498
not in the body of the text. A word or letter in the text that is to be changed should be struck through with a single line: the exact word or letter to be substituted should be written in the margin. When a line of the text is marked in more than one place, the corrections in the margin must appear in order, and be separated from one another by an oblique stroke. All such markings in the margin must consist only of the actual letters or words to be printed; any additional comments or explanations must be ringed. Care should be taken to alter only the minimum number of letters, e.g.

m~~u~~ther o/

not:

~~muther~~ mother/

499 In type, a letter with an accent is a single character. If it is desired to insert an accent in proof, the unaccented letter must be struck out and *the letter with its accent* must be entered in the margin; if, on the contrary, an accent is to be deleted in proof, the accented letter must be struck out and the letter unaccented must be entered in the margin. Similarly, a group of two or three letters joined with a ligature is a single character to the typesetter; if it is wished to take out three separate characters and substitute a ligatured group, the instruction must be made explicit, e.g. by striking out the letters 'f f i' and writing in the margin *[ligatured] ffi*

500 The following table of symbols for correcting proofs includes all those normally required in the reading of proofs of average literary bookwork. Note that, in the extreme left-hand column, the marginal marks set in italics indicate the actual words of instruction to the printer to be written in the margin by the proof corrector. Words in this column set in roman type indicate an instruction to the proof-reader either as to matter to be supplied by him or as to the form which his mark in the margin is to take. The symbol indicating the insertion of space on either side of an en rule is of course also to be used, if desired, with the em rule and the 2-em rule. For symbols used in the correction of mathematical and technical works, British Standard 1219 (see **5** above) should be consulted.
The extract following the table of correction symbols shows the proof marked up with corrections and finally ready for printing. All the errors shown in this extract occur frequently at proof stage, and the recognized correction symbol is shown in each instance. Uncertainty as to the effect of any symbol in the table will be clarified by reference to the text of **494–497**, of which this extract is the proof. The printer's errors are corrected in black ink and new amendments by the author are shown in red.

Symbols for correcting proofs

MARGINAL MARK	MEANING	CORRESPONDING MARK IN TEXT
/	Correction is concluded	None
New matter followed by ⅄	Insert in text the matter indicated in margin	⅄
(/)/	Insert parentheses	⅄ or ⅄⅄
[/]/	Insert brackets	⅄ or ⅄⅄
|-|	Insert hyphen	⅄
ʻ/ ʼ/	Insert single quotation marks	⅄ or ⅄⅄
δ	Delete	Strike through characters to be deleted
δ̂	Delete and close up	Strike through characters to be deleted and use linking marks
#	Delete and leave space	/
stet	Leave as printed	- - - under characters to remain
ital.	Change to italic	— under characters to be altered
s.c.	Change to even small capitals	= under characters to be altered
caps	Change to capital letters	≡ under characters to be altered
c. & s. c.	Change to caps and small caps	≡ under initial letter and = under rest of word(s)

MARGINAL MARK	MEANING	CORRESPONDING MARK IN TEXT
bold	Change to bold type	∿∿ under characters to be altered
l.c.	Change to lower case	Ring characters to be altered
rom.	Change to roman type (from italic)	Ring characters to be altered
med.	Change to medium type (from bold)	Ring characters to be altered
w.f.	Wrong fount	Ring characters to be altered
@	Invert type	Ring characters to be altered
×	Change damaged character(s)	Ring character(s) to be altered
⁐	Close up; delete space between characters. *Also*: Use ligature or diphthong	⁐ linking characters
less #	Reduce space between lines	(connecting lines to be closed up
⅄ under character e.g. $\overset{2}{⅄}$	Substitute or insert character(s) under which this mark is placed, in 'superior' position	/ through character, or ⅄ where appropriate
#	Insert space	/ where appropriate, or > between lines to be spaced
eq #	Make space appear equal between words or letters	/ between words or letters
less #	Reduce space between words	/ between words
trs	Transpose	⊔⊓ between characters or words, numbered when necessary
centre	Place in centre of line	Indicate position with ⌐ ¬

MARGINAL MARK	MEANING	CORRESPONDING MARK IN TEXT
□	Indent one em	⊏ or □
⊏	Move matter to the right	⊏ at left side of group to be moved
⊐	Move matter to the left	⊐ at right side of group to be moved
take over	Take over character(s) or line to next line, column or page	⊏
take back	Take back character(s) or line to previous line, column or page	⊐
═	Straighten lines	═ through lines to be straightened
⊥	Push down space	Ring space affected
n.p.	Begin a new paragraph	□ before the first word of new paragraph
run on	No fresh paragraph here	⁀ between paragraphs
spell out	Spell out the abbreviation or figure in full	Ring words or figures to be altered
⊙/ (,)	Substitute or insert comma	/ through character, or ⋏ where appropriate
⊙/ (:)	Substitute or insert colon	/ through character, or ⋏ where appropriate
⊙/	Substitute or insert full point	/ through characters, or ⋏ where appropriate
<u>*en*</u> /	Insert en rule	⋏
/ <u>*en*</u> \	Insert en rule with space each side	⋏
<u>*em*</u>	Insert em rule	⋏
<u>*2 em*</u>	Insert 2-em rule	⋏

e ∧

bold / 8 /

tis /

take back
run on

If a system of different coloured inks for printer's, editor's,·
and author's corrections is adopted (as suggested above,
429), much unnecessary correspondence is avoided. A fur- *take on*
her refinement of such a system appreciated by printers is
for editor and author to use yet another colour for marking
corrections of actual printer's errors/deviation from the , *en* /
copy as submitted – as [to [opposed] their own second
thoughts. This helps the printer in his accounting he will ⊙ /
not charge his customer for errors made by his own
compositors.

Naturally any such system should be clarified in advance
with all concerned.

© The printer will submit a 'marked set' of proofs together ⅄
with as many spares as the publisher requests. This marked c /
set is precious and should not be used for rough working. = /
l.c. / Publishers usually supply Authors with a duplicate set which
/ can be used for this purpose and also retained for reference.
The publisher's editor will normally collate any other corrections (made by the indexer, the publisher's proof-reader, *take on*
or perhaps an 'outside' specialist reader in the case of a
tis / technical work) on the marked set and ~~decide~~ any final *settle*

queries with the author. The production staff will also wish to check that design instructions have been followed and that no typographical defect remain uncorrected before re-turning the proof, passed press, to the printer. The retention of a 'dummy' reference set (with all corrections marked) in the publisher's office is highly desirable.

The main principle in proof correction is to keep alterations to the minimum and ensure absolute clarity If further material must be inserted every effort should be made to delete or condense other material to make room for it. This som-etimes involves the laborious counting of letters and spaces, but is *much less* costly than upsetting a number off lines, or worse paragraphs or worse still pages. If any matter has to be repaged this will not only be expensive in itself but may also affect the contents list illustrations notes and index. Similarly deleted material should be compensated Handwriting should be unmistakably clear if there is any possibility of error (in reading for instance lovesome' for 'lonesome') the ambiguou sword or phrase should be repeated in block capitals ringed in the outer margin. Any substantial additions should be typed in full.

INDEX

This index is deliberately discursive, so as to provide a concordance as complete as possible. References are to numbered paragraphs.

Index

American College Dictionary, The 1

American–English Usage, A Dictionary of (M. Nicholson) 3

American language: new words in 319; retention of, occasions for 321; un-English usages in 318

American Language, Webster's New World Dictionary of the 1

American usage: capitals in 187, 314; hyphens in 111, 314, 316

American Usage, Modern (W. Follett) 3

ampersand, use of 275, 276

'an' before aspirate 282

'and' linking names of collaborators 64

', and' 20

anglicizing: difficult, examples of 316–20; editor's skill required in 320; responsibility for 313, 315, 320; simple, examples of 315

'anyone' / 'any one' 289

'anyway' / 'any way' 294

apostrophe: clarity as object of 97–9; coined words and 108; decade of years preceded by 109; elimination of 102, 110; elision marked by 100, 107; French proper names and 106; insertion of, when wrong 94, 95, 97, 101; plural *s* and 95, 98, 99, 100; possessive case (sing. and plur.) and 93–6, 103–6, 245; *s* (rom.), following italicized word, and 245; *s* not inserted after, when not pronounced 93, 103; two *s*'s and 93

appendixes: author's 'copy' to include 481; endmatter includes 412; indexing of, necessary 444; running heads for 412

arabic: *see* numerals

article (grammatical): definite, *see* definite article; indefinite, *see* 'a', 'an', *and* indefinite article

articles (periodical), titles of, type for 233, 384

', as a matter of fact,' 37

', as it were,' 37

astronomical terms, caps for 191

Atlas of the British Isles, Complete 2

author, his name on title page 359, 479

authors, names of joint, how linked 63, 64

Authors' and Printers' Dictionary (F. H. Collins) 5

'awhile' / 'a while' 288

'B.C.': extent of years, not to be contracted 230; small caps, to be set in 173; year must precede 229

'Bart': *see* 'Bt'

Bibliographies, subject and national (R. L. Collison) 8

bibliography: accuracy of, important 359; arrangement of 357, 358; articles (signed), how listed in 358, 368, 371–4; articles (unsigned), how listed in 357; author's 'copy' to include 481; bold type in 397;

Index

Index

Index

compass, points of, when to be capitalized 184

compound: adjectives and adverbs, hyphening of 112–15, 117–21, 125, 127, 128; initials in caps or in upper and lower case? 277, 278; letter forms when to be avoided 144, 305; letters not to be divided 255, 420; nouns, hyphening of 122–5; sentences 35; words, how to be divided 432; words referring to Deity, whether to be capitalized 178–80

Concise Oxford Dictionary of Current English, The 1

consistency: author's 'copy' must show 483; bibliographical 367, 377; hyphenation must have 153; index copy to be prepared with scrupulous 486; spellings (alternative) to be chosen with 306; transliteration must observe 322

contents, list of: index to appear in 451; prelims to include 411, 479

contractions: abbreviations distinguished from 107, 263; full point when to follow 267; recommended 211–12, 230, 349; rules against 213, 226, 230, 231, 399

conversation: *see* dialogue

'copy' (author's): additions to, how to be inserted 477; amendments to 489, 490; carbon copies of handwritten matter in, important 473; cross-references to be inserted in 485; double-space typing recommended for 475; footnotes in, recommended style for 475; handwriting inadvisable in 472; headings to be clear in 483; inks (various) used in 489; instructions to printer, how presented in 491; italic type, how to be indicated in 484; manuscript alterations to 478; margins in 475, 478; photocopies of handwritten 473; preparation of 313, 314, 471, 492; quoted matter in, how indicated 475; three copies of, desirable 472; unique documents in, care of 474

corrigenda: *see* errata

cross-references: author's 'copy' 485; index 449

' 'd' (contraction), distinguished from 'd' ' (abbreviation) 107

' 'd', ' 'ed' (suffix) 108

Daily Mail, chosen style of transliteration to be respected 327

dashes: colons not to be followed by 47, 56; haphazard use of 42, 54; paired to form parenthesis 55; punctuation marks (other) and 57

date, expressions of: comma often superfluous in 226; days of month not to be contracted in 231; division of, to be avoided 427; en rule's misuse in 228; lining figures when preferable in 199; small caps in 173, 229, 230; years when to be contracted in 230

'de' (French): capitalized in English and American names 251; lower case normal for 250

decimal: coinage 9, 217; number 217, 218

decorations, type for 170, 172

Index

Index

Index

foreword: *see* preface

Forsyte Saga, The (J. Galsworthy), suitable for indexing 437

fount, choice of, important 197, 198, 252, 408

fractions: between 1 and 2 219; hyphening of spelt-out 145

French names 136, 140, 142, 250

French words, ligature to be retained in 305

full points: abbreviations normally ended by 9, 264, 274, 275, 279; contractions rarely ended by 267; dates', set between numbers 223, 350; decimal coinage's use of 9, 217; ellipses when preceded by 12; final, when omitted in notes 347; 'leaders' formed of 15; omission of 10, 277, 279; parentheses enclosing 14, 74; parentheses excluding 14, 73; raised, used in decimal numbers 217; relation of, to final quote 157–8; wrong use of 16

galley proofs 439, 482

Gazetteer of the British Isles 2

gazetteers 2

Geographical Dictionary, Webster's 2, 325

geographical divisions, caps for 184

geographical names, in various languages 256

Geographical Society, Royal, authoritative on transliteration 325

geological terms, caps for 191

German names 250, 252–3

glossary 6, 7; author's 'copy' to include 481; endmatter normally includes 412, 481; index may incorporate 7, 446, 455; prelims may conveniently include 411

Greek, words derived from 305, 310

Greek words, indexing of 442, 454

'half-' 146

half-titles 10, 479

hanging figures: *see* figures, non-lining

headings, system of, to be uniform throughout author's 'copy' 483

headlines: endmatter to be given distinctive 412; endnotes to be provided with 334–5, 378; full point to be omitted from 10; left- and right-hand, distinguished 409, 411, 412, 482; non-lining figures suitable for 201; omitted from first pages of chapters 410; running, for prelims 411; shortened 482; specification of, before page-proof stage 482

Herrick, Robert, quoted 298

historical persons: obscure 2; successions of 2

honours 41, 172

hotels, names of, type for 234

houses, names of great: shortened 239; type for 234

'however' / 'how ever' 293

Index

hyphen(s): accurate placing of, important 130; American usage too sparing of 111; American use of, contrasted with English 111, 314, 316; compound words joined by 112–15, 117–25, 127–9; consistent use of, important 153; diaeresis secondary to 260; discretion necessary in use of 111, 116, 148, 150, 153, 209; en rule distinguished from 60–2, 65, 210, 211, 212, 215; English taste in 111, 149, 260; 'fellow' when followed by 147–8; forenames including 65, 140; fractions incorporate, when spelt out 145; French use of, in names 65, 136, 140, 142; 'half' when followed by 145, 146; letters, identical and adjacent, to be separated by 132; lines ending in, not to exceed two in succession 418; misuse of 60, 62, 116, 215; multiple use of, to be reduced 209, 433; place names, French, with or without? 136; prefix and cap separated by 133; presence and absence of, contrasted 112, 115–16, 118, 120, 126, 127, 131, 134, 136, 137–9, 145, 146, 147–8, 149, 152; rules on, difficult to formulate 111, 153; '*Saint*(*e*)' when followed by 136, 141, 142; suffix when to be preceded by 134; surnames, double, without 138, 141, 303; surnames including 137, 139, 142, 303; time, expressions of, and 143, 145; typographical need for 144; vagaries of 152; variable part of word introduced or followed by 135, 187

'ibid.' 264, 272; correctly used 392; meaning of 388; misuse of 389, 390

Icelandic words, ligature to be retained in 305

'id.' 264, 272; correctly used 389; meaning of 388

'i.e.' 272; comma in relation to 33

ij (Dutch), not to be divided 255, 420

illustrations: foot folios to be omitted under full-page 407; footnotes not to be interrupted by 338; index to include 444; indicated by italic numerals in index 469; prelims to include list of 411, 479; preparation of, by author 487–8; words not to be divided by 416

illustrator: right of, to be named in work 441; title page may include name of 479

inconsistency rarely justified 98

', indeed,', parenthetical use of 39

indefinite article: avoidance of, in index entry 453; form of 280–2

indention, degree of, in quoted matter 161; *see also* quoted extracts

index: accuracy of, essential 439, 458; adequate time to be allowed for compilation of 438–9; alphabetical arrangement of 450, 452–4, 456–7; articles, definite and indefinite, to be placed at end of entries 453; author ideally responsible for 438; bold type, how used in 469; clarity to be aimed at throughout 457, 461, 463–4; colon, how used in 459, 463; columns of, usually two or three 440, 464; comma, how used in 461, 463; compilation of, skilled job 438, 450; concordance

index (*contd*)
may be incorporated in 440; contents list to include 451; copy preparation of 486; cross-referencing in 449; early compilation of, to be encouraged 439; economic value of 435; endmatter normally includes 412; enjoyment of work revived by reading of 435; entries, specimens of 453–6, 461, 463, 470; fictional works may benefit by 437; glossarial 7, 446, 455; illustrations to be included in 444, 469; indention of subentries etc. in 463–4; initial letter of entry normally lower-case 466; italic type, how used in 464, 468, 469; key-words, their importance in 447–8; length of, varied 440; more than one, when necessary 442, 445, 452; most works in need of 435; non-roman script to be included in 443, 454; numerals to be included in 454; omission of, a crime 436; one, normally sufficient 442; plates to be included in 469; position of 412, 451; preliminary note to, content of 442, 452, 457, 469–70; prelims may include 451; principles of compilation of, to be explained 452, 469–70; purchase of work may be decided by 435; reference system of, to be explained 452, 470; roman numerals, how used in 469; running headlines for 412; semicolon, how used in 460; small caps not recommended in 467; space necessary to secure clarity of 461, 463, 467; subentries in 457, 459, 460–1, 463–4; sub-subentries in 463–4; symbols to be included in 443, 454; type used in, to be explained 452, 469; type-size suitable for 465; typescript, possible compilation from 439

Index, Making an (G. V. Carey) 5

indexer: adequate time to be allowed for work of 439; credit to, by name 441; duties of 447–9; imagination required of 446–7; topics of interest to be noted by 447; value of, at proof stage 493, 495

Indexers, Society of 5, 438

indirect question 86

initial letters, words composed of 277, 280

inns, names of, type for 234

introduction, as part of preliminary matter 479

inversion of sentence, comma not required in 18

'-ise' endings 1, 307; complete list of obligatory 311

italic type: author's 'copy' to contain indication of 484; editorial introduction of, to be marked 247; emphasis marked by 247; foreign words normally in 240; index use of 468; Latin abbreviations when to be set in 244; punctuation when to be set in 85, 92, 249; restraint in use of 54, 247; roman type, relation of, to 96; Scripture book titles when to be set in 402; single letter or word when to be set in 246; titles of literary works, to be set in 232, 235–9, 468

'its' 94

'-ize' ending 307–10

'jun.' 264; comma superfluous before 41

Karadjordjević, Aleksandar, correct spelling of 326

Khrushchev, Nikita Sergeevich, correctly transliterated 327

'£', without following full point 274

Landes, D. S. *Bankers and Pashas* 355

Latin words 305; as abbreviations 244

' 'ld', former contraction for 'would' 107

'leaders': defined 15; 2-point groups preferred in 15

length, hyphening in expressions of 129

ligature: hyphen preferred to 144; insertion of, in proof correction 499; retention of, in certain languages 305

ll (Spanish, Welsh) not to be divided 420

'loc. cit.' 272; correct use of 387, 392

lower-case type: abbreviations in 272, 346; caps' use distinguished from 171, 176, 178–82, 184, 185–6, 189, 192, 193–4; caps when not preferred to 49, 82, 194; colon when followed by 49; dates' roman numerals in 223, 349, 350; Deity, when references to, are in 179–82; full point followed by 82; notes recommended to be in 223, 272, 346, 349; prefixes to proper names set in 250; roman numerals when in 223, 349, 403, 406, 480; seasons when in 185–6; sentence can begin with certain abbreviations in 272; titles of address in 174; volume numbers' roman numerals in 223

'Mac', 'Mc', 'M' ', indexing of 456

magazines: *see* periodicals

Making of a Book, The (G. A. Campbell) 7

marks of reference: *see* reference

measurement: hyphened nouns of 129; statistics of, figures to be used for 207

Megarry, R. E. *Miscellany-at-Law*, index to 440

Mind the Stop (G. V. Carey) 4

musical compositions, titles of shorter, type for 233

musical symbols, indexing of 454–5

names 41, 63–5; abbreviated, to have no final full point 268; classical and biblical 104; foreign 106, 250, 252–6; sovereigns' 224; style of, to accord with bearers' personal usage 251, 304; *see also* forenames, surnames

natural history, terms of, how capitalized 192

'near-' 125

'Negro', to be capitalized 183

newspapers, titles of: definite article part of 235; italic type to be used for 232; shortened 239; without definite article 236; *see also* periodicals

Index

'no', when capitalized 188

non-roman script: indexing of 443, 454; transliteration of 322

notes: abbreviations and contractions to be used in 349; bibliography to precede 354; chapters not so conveniently followed by 335; endnotes (q.v.) or footnotes (q.v.) 332; indication of, in text 329; lower case to be used in 223, 346, 349; punctuation of 347–9; specimens of 350; supplementary to text 328

nouns: compounded with adjectives 112–13; compounded with numbers 129; compounded with participles 120; hyphening of 122–5

numbers: compounded with adjectives 128; compounded with nouns 129; decimal 217–18; extent of 60–1, 210–15, 399; figures when to be used to express 203, 204, 209, 210, 216; house- , not to be followed by comma 221; multi-figure, commas to be inserted in 220; precise, to be expressed in figures 207; round, when to be spelt out 205; sequences of 210, 211–13; spelt out, when to be 202, 205, 208, 210, 216

numerals: arabic 399, 404, 406; en rule when to be used to join 60; indexing of 454; roman, *see* roman numerals; shortened 109

'O', use of, in vocative case 283

'œ' 305

', of course,': commas sometimes unnecessary in 38; parenthetical use of 37

'Oh', as expression of emphasis 284

Old English words, ligature to be retained in 305

'op. cit.' 272; care necessary in use of 386, 391

operas, titles of: shortened 239; type for 232

oratorios, titles of: shortened 239; type for 232

'p.m.', numerals to be used with 216

Paderewski, Ignacy Jan, correct spelling of 326

page numbers: author's 'copy' to include 476; bibliography, when to be given in 368, 375, 379; cross-reference, when inserted 485; foot of page occasionally to bear 408; omission of 407, 408

page proofs, page references to be entered in 485, 492

pagination 386, 403–8; expense of revising 496; prelims', in author's 'copy' 480

paintings, titles of, type for 233

pamphlets 5, 6, 8

paperbacks 1, 3, 4, 7; bibliography should note 364

parentheses: bibliographical use of 350, 363, 364, 366–73, 377, 380, 383, 385, 397, 398; brackets contrasted with 72, 77; exclamation mark within 83; pairs of, usual 72; punctuation marks' relation to 73–6; question mark within 90

Index

Index

publication details: parentheses for 366; shortening of, permissible in bibliography 360; title page to include 479

publisher's editor, duties of 313, 483, 495

publishers' names, form of, in bibliography 360

punctuation: American 4; bibliographical use of 1–8, 348, 363, 365, 366, 367, 370, 373, 376; italicizing of marks of, when permissible 249; 'Oh' usually followed by mark of 284; restraint of 347, 349, 361; style contributed to by 54; superior marks of reference and 330–1; typographical change as substitute for 361

quantities: *see* comparative quantities

question: exclamation mark may follow 89; unquoted, introduced by colon 48

question mark: affirmative sentence may be followed by 88; indirect question not to be followed by 86; italicizing of, care required in 92; questions not requiring 87, 89; sceptical use of 90–1

quotation: colon to introduce 46–7; comma to introduce 47; exact, importance of 247, 327

quotation marks: *see* quotes

Quotations, The Concise Oxford Dictionary of 2

Quotations, The Oxford Dictionary of 2

quoted extracts: brackets in introduction of 163; colon introducing 46–7, 168; comma introducing 32, 47, 164, 168; ellipsis at beginning of 166; indention of 161; lengthy, to be indented 161, 475; matter following, normally set full out 162; punctuation preceding, to be normal 165, 168; separation of, from footnote by rule 337; typesize of, when indented 161, 167; verse, treatment of 167, 169; wrong use of colon to introduce 164

'quoted from . . .' 346

quotes: colloquial terms in 155; comma when unnecessary after 159; double, normally used within single 154; final, set at end of last paragraph only 160; indented matter not enclosed in 161, 167; marks of reference, how related to 330; omission of, in unspoken dialogue 156; phrases when set in 155; punctuation marks within or outside? 157–8; repeated at opening of each paragraph 160; quoted matter within verse extract to be enclosed in 169; single, normally used 154; single, when used within double 154; single words when set in 155; titles of works when in 233; verse extract (indented) not to be enclosed in 167

ranging: footnotes require 343–5; paragraphs (numbered) need care in 225

ranks 170

ratio, expressions of 50

're-' 131, 423

Index

reading, aids to: apostrophe 99; book lists 356; comma 19, 30; division of words 422–3; notes 328; position of bibliography 353

reading, obstructions to: commas 17–18; dashes 54; footnotes 378

reference, marks of: conventional, distinguished from superior figures 329, 334, 339; footnotes alone introduced by 333–4, 339; illustrated 329; position of, in relation to punctuation marks 330–1; *see also* superior (figure)

references: arabic numerals' use in 399; articles (periodical), their style of 383–5; bold type's use in 397; brevity desirable in 379, 381–2; clarity of, essential 379, 386, 387, 394, 396, 402; comma when to be omitted in 220; conciseness desirable in 336, 355; English, preferred to Latin 394; Latin, if used, to be used correctly 393; location of, to be made easy 335, 353, 358, 378; numbered verse lines' 220; particulars to be given in 379; position of, on page or at end of work 333–4, 336, 378; repeated, style to be followed in 381–2, 384, 385–92; Scriptural 279, 399–402; shortened 239, 381–2, 384–5, 395; specimens of 380–5, 389–92, 395, 397–8; text matter not to be repeated in 380; typography of 379, 395, 397

regimental histories, problems of 170

rhetorical use of em rule 68

Roget, P. M. *Thesaurus of English Words and Phrases* 1

roman alphabet, not to be transliterated 326

roman numerals: caps unnecessary for 223–4, 349, 358; dates' use of 223, 350; lower case for 214, 223, 349, 350, 358, 370, 372, 373, 385, 395, 398, 403, 406, 480; notes' 349–50; numbers' extent in 214; small caps for 224, 350, 358, 383, 395; volume numbers' 223, 358

roman type: foreign words when to be set in 241–3, 248; Latin abbreviations set in 244; possessive 's', after word in italic, to be set in 245; punctuation marks when to be set in 249; words, normally italicized, when to be set in 248

rule necessary to separate footnote from text: in author's 'copy' 475; in print 337

Rules for Compositors and Readers (H. Hart) 5

rules of thumb, erroneous 18, 236n.

running headlines: *see* headlines

Ruskin, Works of John (ed. Cook & Wedderburn), index-concordance to 440

' 's', in roman type, after word in italic 245

', say,' 37

Scandinavian words, ligature to be retained in 305

Scripture references 213; clarity in 402; indexing of 442

sculptures, titles of, type for 233

seasons 185–6

Index

Index

suffix: '-ize' as a 308–9; word-division to be avoided for 419, 424

superior (figure): distinguished from conventional mark of reference 329, 334, 339; endnotes referred to by 334; footnotes may be referred to by 339; fount of, to be same in notes as in text 339; punctuation marks and 330–1; *see also* reference

surnames, double: hyphened 137, 142; uncertainly hyphened 139; unhyphened 138, 141

symbols: index can include 443, 454–5; list of, included in end-matter 412; monetary, style of 274; prelims may include list of 479; reference to notes by means of 329; undesirable in general writing 273; *see also* ampersand, '%', solidus

symphonies, titles of, type for 233

' 't' (Dutch), how to be set 254

tabular matter, setting of 199, 273, 416

Taylor, A. J. P. *English History 1914–1945*, index to 440

Telephone Directory not infallible 276

telephone numbers, omission of comma in 220

theatres, names of: shortened 239; type for 234

', then,', parenthetical use of 40

time: clock- 216, 427; expressions of 129, 143; extent of 60, 129, 213

Times Atlas, The 2

Times Index-Gazetteer of the World, The 2, 325

title page: authentic source of bibliographical details 359; contents of 479; full points normally omitted from 10

titles (of works): abbreviated, rules for setting 239; caps, how to use for 195; definite article excluded from 236, 238; definite article part of 235; foreign, setting of 196; italic type, when to use for 232; roman type quoted, when to use for 233; Scriptural, when to italicize 402; translated 196; *see also* short titles

titles (personal): English, of address 174; foreign, of address 243; honorific 172; hyphened 177; noble 243, 303

Tom Jones (Fielding), suitable for indexing 437

', too,', parenthetical use of 39

trade-names 193

trains, names of, type for 234

translator: bibliography to include name of 358, 365; right of, to be named in work 441; title page should include name of 479

transliteration: accuracy of, important 322; authorities on 325; English sounds to be reproduced in 322; faulty, can be offensive 324; incorrect forms of, established by usage 256, 323; roman script no subject for 326; simpler though incorrect forms of, sometimes indulged in 327; specimens of correct 323; standards of, vary 325

Index